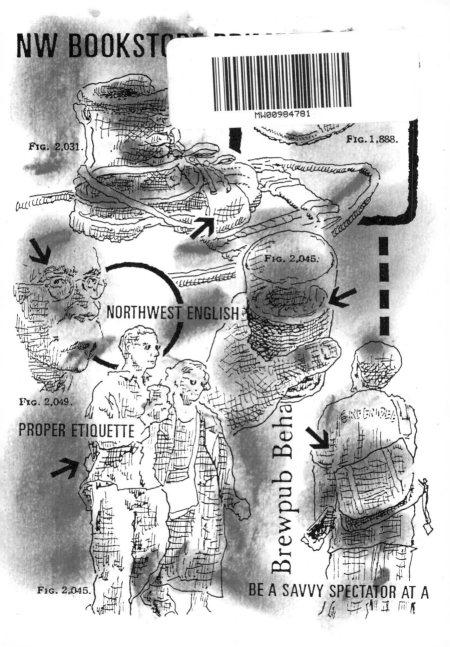

NW BOOKSTORE

FIG. 2,031.

FIG. 1,888.

FIG. 2,045.

NORTHWEST ENGLISH

FIG. 2,049.

PROPER ETIQUETTE

FIG. 2,045.

Brewpub Beha

BE A SAVVY SPECTATOR AT A

NORTHWEST BASIC TRAINING

ESSENTIAL SKILLS
for
VISITORS, NEWCOMERS,
& NATIVE NORTHWESTERNERS

TEXT BY
GREG EIDEN

Illustrated with
Diagrams and Pictures

BY
KURT D. HOLLOMON

Photographs

BY
DEBRA SHISHKOFF

This book belongs to:

. . . .

. . . .
NORTHWEST RANK
(VISITOR, NEWCOMER, OR NATIVE)

SASQUATCH BOOKS
SEATTLE

TEXT AND EXTENSIVE RESEARCH | **GREG EIDEN**
DESIGN AND ILLUSTRATION | **KURT D. HOLLOMON**
COMPOSITION AND CREATIVE CONSULTANT | **DEBRA SHISHKOFF**

Library of Congress Cataloging in Publication
Eiden, Greg.
    Northwest basic training : essential skills for
visitors, newcomers, and native Northwesterners
/ by Greg Eiden ; illustrated with diagrams and
pictures by Kurt D. Hollomon.
    p. cm.
ISBN 1-57061-309-5
1. Northwest, Pacific–Guidebooks. 2. Northwest,
Pacific–Social life and customs–Humor. I.
Hollomon, Kurt D. II. Title.
F852.3.E38 2001
917.95004'44–dc21 2001042956

PUBLISHED BY

SASQUATCH BOOKS

615 Second Avenue Seattle, WA 98104
www.sasquatchbooks.com books@sasquatchbooks.com

INTRODUCTION

The following pages contain many of the essential skills necessary for life in America's upper west corner. You'll find sound advice, pretty sound advice, and even some advice that's a bit tongue-in-cheek. At first glance, the chapters may seem a bit random. Closer inspection reveals that indeed they are. That's because we Northwesterners love a bit of chaos in life. You see it in how we dress. In the way we decorate. In our music. Chaos is good. Challenging the long-established norms of North American living is our heritage.

You'll notice that we've divided the book into three sections.

– VISITOR –

Anyone smart enough to plan a trip to the Northwest corner of America.

– NEWCOMER –

Anyone smart enough to move to the Northwest corner of America.

– NATIVE NORTHWESTERNER –

Anyone smart enough to spend their life in the Northwest corner of America.

Don't forget to leave your copy of *Northwest Basic Training* on your peeled-timber, hand-carved, red cedar end table for others to enjoy. Now sit back, pour yourself a double-tall latte, and start reading.

CONTENTS

SECTION No. 1 — ESSENTIAL SKILLS FOR THE VISITOR

HOW TO PREPARE FOR YOUR NORTHWEST VISIT
.... **1** ....

SECTION No. 2	NEWCOMERS A PRIMER

HOW TO GET ACCLIMATED TO YOUR NEW SURROUNDINGS
. . . . **55** . . . .

SECTION *No. 3* — **NATIVE NORTHWESTERNER**

SECTION
No. 1

ESSENTIAL SKILLS
FOR THE VISITOR

You are planning to visit relatives or friends. Or, perhaps you just have the uncommon good sense to get away from it all to one of the great parts of the world. Rest assured, there are periods of time during the year when it won't rain. Once you've chosen one of those three days, start getting ready.

Planning

TWO WEEKS BEFORE LEAVING

- ❏ Read *Sometimes a Great Notion* aloud.
- ❏ Increase caffeine intake by 50%.
- ❏ Increase National Public Radio intake by 50%.
- ❏ Order waterproof, breathable rain gear.

ONE WEEK BEFORE LEAVING

- ❏ Begin drinking caffeine at night.
- ❏ Hug a tree.
- ❏ Read Stihl catalog.
- ❏ Take shower with your clothes on to acclimate yourself.

TWO DAYS BEFORE LEAVING

- ❏ Waterproof golf shoes.
- ❏ Practice wine-tasting "swirl."
- ❏ Pack small, medium, and large umbrellas.
- ❏ Buy *Undaunted Courage* to read on trip.

LAST MINUTE—TWO HOURS BEFORE LEAVING

- ❏ If flying, check flight times for fog delays.
- ❏ If driving, fill gas tank (last chance to gas up car at decent price).
- ❏ Optimistically double check supply of sunscreen.
- ❏ Apply "Oregon or Bust" stickers to luggage.

CHAPTER 1
LEARN TO SPEAK
PROPER NW ENGLISH

– ASH –
Product of Mount St. Helens.

– BEAV –
Student at Oregon State University.

– BLACK ICE –
An invisible menace: ice
on pavement.

– BUGABOO –
A) Mountain chain in
British Columbia;
B) Columbia Sportswear parka.

– BUGLE –
The sound a bull elk makes
during rut.

– BUMBERSHOOT –
A) Umbrella;
B) Seattle's annual Labor Day
arts and music fest.

– CHINOOK –
A) Native American tribe;
B) Alternative name for king salmon.

– COUGAR –
A) Mountain lion;
B) Student at Washington
State University.

– DUCK –
Student at University of Oregon.

– EBB –
Outgoing tide.

– LADDER –
Device to help salmon
"climb" over dams.

– GEODUCK –
Pronounced "GOO-ey-duck."
A gargantuan,
bizarre-looking clam.

– GREENER –
A) Environmentalist;
B) Student at Evergreen College.

– HANK –
Affectionate slang for popular
local beer, Henry Weinhard's.

– HUSKY –
Student at U-Dub.

– MOLLYHUGGER –
Scary monsters that live in the hills
around Northwest camping areas.

– MOUNTAIN'S OUT –

Seattlese for that rare moment when the clouds part enough to afford a view of Mount Rainier.

– NUKE WINDS –

Winds that blow down the Columbia River Gorge from the Hanford Reach, causing windsurfers to become wildly excited.

– NUTRIA –

Pest imported from South America.

– OLY –

A brew from Washington's capitol city, Olympia.

– ORCA –

Killer whale.

– OREGON –

Pronounced "OR-eh-gun." Only imposters say "OR-e-GONE."

– PUYALLUP –

Pronounced "Pew-AL-up." Tongue-twisting Washington city.

– REEDIE –

Alumnus of, or student at, Portland's Reed College.

– SEAHAWK –

A)Member of Seattle pro-football team;
B)Northwest raptor aka osprey.

– SILVER THAW –

Rain frozen on branches, power lines, etc.

– SLACK –

Period of time at the turn of the tide, either high or low.

– SLUG –

Ubiquitous, slime-producing, land-dwelling gastropod.

– STEELHEAD –

Ocean-run rainbow trout.

– TREE HUGGER –

Committed environmentalist.

– U-DUB –

The University of Washington.

– WEBFOOT –

Native Northwesterner.

– WILLAMETTE –

Pronounced "Will-AM-et." River that flows through Portland.

– ZAG –

Short for Gonzaga University of basketball fame.

> CHAPTER 2
> **HOW TO**
> **BREAK THE ICE**

Ten proven ways to start a conversation
with a Northwesterner

1. MAKE FUN OF L.A.—Crowds, smog, car-jackings, fires, Hollywood types—all these are the antithesis of the Northwest. **2. MENTION THE GRAY SKIES**— Fog and rain are consistent conversational springboards. Or try this line: "Does anyone know the difference between El Niño and La Niña?" **3. ACT INTERESTED IN HIGH TECH**—Half the people you'll meet here work with software or chips. **4. ASK ABOUT GEODUCKS**— and other distinctive local fauna. The bizarre clam known as a geoduck has a 12-inch foot with a startling resemblance to a different appendage. Mentioning other strange creatures such as Sasquatch (aka Bigfoot) and sturgeon shows you're in the know. **5. TALK TRASH ABOUT SLUGS**—Goofy antennae. Spineless. Slimy. 'Nuff said. **6. SAY ANYTHING COFFEE**—Bemoan the latest jump in coffee bean prices. Or toss out a comment on the latest coffee you've tried: "The Sulawese blend was *amazing*. Have you tried it?" **7. INQUIRE ABOUT OPEN AIR MARKETS**—Northwesterners not only like to shop in markets without walls, they like to talk about them. What's good, what's ripe, where the bargains are. **8. NAME-DROP ANY NORTHWEST SPORTS TEAM**— Choose any team named after an animal: Beavers, Ducks, Cougars, Huskies, etc. **9. PRETEND TO BE A SAILBOARDER**—Everyone's fascinated by it, but no one actually does it. So feel free to fake expertise. **10. TALK MUSIC, AVOID GRUNGE**—The regional scene runs from edgy rock to blues and jazz.

CHAPTER 3
MASTER THE OCEAN BEACH BASICS

Stay safe while beachcombing

(**1**) Keep children off logs. Logs rolled by ocean surf can be deadly. When a wave rolls a log, it becomes an unstoppable force than can crush or pin a limb. (**2**) Watch for sneaker waves. Aptly named, these rogue waves sneak in unexpectedly, knocking you off your feet. They may also carry logs. (**3**) Be cautious with beach fires. Some areas require beach fires to be

50 feet from dunes, whose fragile grasses ignite easily. Douse campfires with water, rake, cover with 6 inches of sand and rake again.

Win a sandcastle building contest: cheat

(1) In four 5-gallon pails, mix 10 parts beach sand and 1 part Elmer's glue. **(2)** Set mixtures aside. **(3)** Dig wet sand and pour into precut plywood form designed to emulate the Taj Mahal. **(4)** Repeat for second, third, and fourth levels. **(5)** Coat outside of plywood forms with glue-laden sand to hide from judges. **(6)** As you walk to restroom for break, "accidentally" stumble over driftwood and careen into opponent's sand sculpture.

Know when to walk the beach

Buy a tide table. It'll show you whether the beach you plan to visit will be exposed or will be buried under several feet of seawater.

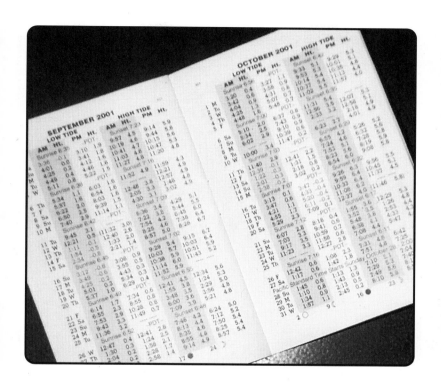

Sample Tide Table

If you want to dig clams or explore tide pools, time your visit for a minus tide. The larger the negative number, the lower the tide.

Identify your beachcombing treasures

SAND DOLLAR (BETTER THAN A SAND HALF-DOLLAR)

KEYHOLE LIMPET

GLASS FISHING FLOAT

FOSSILIZED SCALLOP SHELL (MIOCENE ERA)

FOSSILIZED OLYMPIA BEER CAN ('70S ERA)

CRABSHELL

DRIFTWOOD

AGATE

REDHOOK ESB BOTTLE

GREAT WHITE SHARK TOOTH

CHANNELED DOG WHELK

NIKES (FROM 1990S CARGO SPILL)

BABY SEAL

Choose Pacific wind protection

LIP BALM

SUNSCREEN
EVEN IF THE SUN ISN'T OUT SUNSCREEN PROTECTS AGAINST WINDBURN.

BEACH UMBRELLA
DOUBLES AS ITEM OF SPORTS EQUIPMENT WHEN WIND PICKS IT UP AND YOU HAVE TO CHASE IT DOWN THE BEACH.

CAUTION: Approaching baby seals on beach may cause mother to abandon them.

CHAPTER 4
**PROPER ETIQUETTE
FOR GETTING NAKED**

Natural hot springs (often enjoyed au naturel*) dot
the Northwest. Please observe the following rules:*

1. If hot spring is already occupied when you arrive,
   use discretion regarding attire. If everyone
   else is wearing a bathing suit, wear yours.

2. If everyone else is naked, you may as
   well get naked.

3. If there's no one else around, you may
   as well get naked.

4. On weekends, the bodies present are
   likely to be young and supple. If yours
   isn't, you may want to reconsider #2.

5. No glass containers in hot springs.
   Broken glass and bare genitals do not mix.

6. Always test hot springs with a finger or toe.
   An ideal temperature is 100°–108°F. Geothermal
   activity may heat pools to 180°.

7. Leave the hot spring area the way you found it.
   Don't leave trash behind.

NOTE: Ignore the feeling that someone is watching you while you bathe. Many thermal spring areas are populated by sharp-eyed eagles.

8. Don't disrobe in the parking lot. Some are near the highway, and the sight of your body could cause an accident.

CHAPTER 5
HOW BUMPER STICKERS REVEAL WHAT'S ON THE CAR RADIO

– SPOTTED OWL STEW SERVED HERE –
Old country

– RAAAAIIIINNNNNIIIIEEEEER BEER –
New country

— MAKE LOVE, NOT LUMBER —
NPR

— NUKE FREE ZONE —
Bonnie Raitt

— I HAVE 'SHROOMS ON THE BRAIN —
Phish

— WHO NEEDS BALLS? GO RAFTING —
Dixie Chicks

— THIS CAR PROTECTED BY SMITH & WESSON —
Rush Limbaugh

CHAPTER 6
**HOW TO BLEND IN
AT A COFFEEHOUSE**

1. Order quickly and knowingly. Let your order roll off your tongue in a confident burst.
2. Order coffee du jour by name—e.g., "I'd like the Ethiopian blend, please."
3. Always toss your change into the tip jar. Baristas are underpaid.

4. Observe the body language of the person in front of you. General antsiness or hunched shoulders suggest "Move it along, nobody has time to chat." Casual shrugs, laughs, or direct smiles suggest "I'd love to give you a few tips on good restaurants in the area."

5. Purchase "travel mug" with the understanding that it comes filled with coffee. Don't ask.

6. Pay with $10 bill so you don't have to ask the price of your exotic drink.

7. Gaze knowingly at teas, but don't buy. This is, after all, a coffeehouse.

8. Order an iced drink only when outside temperature rises above 80°.

9. Never walk off with the house reading materials.

Practice order
"Vanilla double tall
skinny
two cup, please."

Translation
"I'd like two shots
of espresso in
my vanilla latte,
12-ounce size,
with a second cup
to protect my
delicate hands."

Coffeehouse lingo

BARISTA. Professional espresso drink maker.

CAPPUCINO. Espresso with foamed milk.

DOPPIO. A fun way to say "A double shot of espresso, please."

DOUBLE TALL. A 12-oz. drink with a double shot of espresso.

ESPRESSO. The very strong Italian coffee brew.

GRANDE. Means "large," but gets you only a medium—a 16-oz. drink.

HALF CAF. Drink made with half caffeinated and half decaffeinated coffee. For the truly indecisive person.

JAVA JACKET. Pinky protector to wrap around your hot cup.

JAVA JUNKY. Coffee lover.

JOE. A waiter in Yakima. Also slang for coffee.

LATTE. Espresso with steamed milk, topped with half an inch of milk foam.

MOCHA. Latte with chocolate, may be topped with whipped cream.

SKINNY. Espresso drink made with nonfat milk.

TALL. "Tall" equals "small." A 12-oz. drink.

TWO CUP. A request that the barista double-cup your hot beverage.

UNLEADED. Decaffeinated.

VANILLA LATTE. One of a variety of flavored lattes.

WHY BOTHER. Decaffeinated latte made with nonfat milk.

WITH ROOM. "Please leave room for cream."

1. Visit tasting room right at the winery.

2. Casually approach the vintner and ask which varietals are being tasted.

3. He/she should offer to start you with one of the dry white wines, such as chardonnay.

4. Be sure to swirl wine in the glass.

5. Smell your wine before sipping.

   CAUTION: Commenting on the "bouquet," or aroma, is too advanced. Just smell and smile knowingly.

6. Move on to the more complex red wines—the Merlots or Pinot Noirs.

7. Always cleanse your palate with a cracker between tastings.

8. Finish with the sweetest wines being tasted, such as a Riesling or a dessert wine. This way the sugars and acids in the sweeter wines won't cause the dry wines to seem too astringent.

9. Make pithy comments as you taste:
"This Pinot has aged well...I detect a hint of earthy spices." OR *"The Sauvignon Blanc is a bit crisp for my taste, but I admire the citrus overtones."* OR *"Is this the earliest Merlot vintage you're tasting today?"*

10. Never feel compelled to finish all the wine in your tasting glass. After all, you may visit several wineries in one afternoon.

How to Read a Northwest Wine Label

1. WINERY NAME

2. VINTAGE
(YEAR THE GRAPES WERE HARVESTED; TYPICALLY, WINE MUST CONTAIN 95% OF GRAPES FROM STATED YEAR).

3. STATE OF ORIGIN

4. VARIETAL
(NAME OF GRAPE OR OF WINE MADE FROM THAT GRAPE—E.G., CHARDONNAY).

5. AVA
(AMERICAN VITICULTURAL AREA, AKA APPELLATION. THE GRAPES' DESIGNATED GROWING REGION).

Match the Northwest food to the Northwest wine

1. roasted hazelnuts   **A.** Chardonnay

2. clams   **B.** Pinot Noir

3. oysters   **C.** Merlot

4. salmon   **D.** Cabernet Sauvignon

5. sautéed duck breasts   **E.** Pinot Gris

6. dungeness crab   **F.** Riesling

7. pear/walnut salad   **G.** Sauvignon Blanc

8. mushroom dishes

KEY: 1-A, 2-G or F, 3-G or F, 4-A, or B, 5-C, 6-E or G, 7-F, 8-D

CHAPTER 8
HOW TO MASTER A NORTHWEST SEAFOOD MENU

– OYSTER SHOOTER –

Aka oyster-on-the-half-shell. Slurp, chew, and swallow it raw.

– STURGEON –

A million years old, yet it's not even tough. A Northwest delicacy.

– HALIBUT –

The fish may be flat, but the flavor is well rounded.

– BAY SHRIMP –

Tiny shrimp, the kind you typically find on a salad.

– PRAWNS –

Big ol' juicy, tasty shrimps. May be steamed or deep-fried.

– STEAMERS –

Littleneck clams or butterclams, steamed until they open;
usually served in their own juices with butter and garlic.

– FISH AND CHIPS, COD –

The traditional English working-class meal, but in the Northwest
your order doesn't come wrapped in newspaper.

– FISH AND CHIPS, HALIBUT –

Same, but made with the more flavorful halibut and
with a higher price attached.

– KING SALMON –

The king of tastes, a deep red meat packed with healthy fatty acids.
The largest Pacific salmon. Aka Chinook.

– COHO SALMON –

Aka silver salmon. A smaller species, with pink meat.

– CRAB CAKES –

A Puget Sound legend that rivals–and some say exceeds–
the cakes served back East.

– CIOPPINO –

A thick, tomato-based fish stew jammed with crab, clams,
scallops, fish, and/or prawns.

– CLAM CHOWDER –

Almost all clam chowder you'll find in the Northwest is New England style—the white kind made with milk and cream. The best chowders have nice big chunks of clam and lots of 'em.

– DUNGENESS CRAB –

The big, succulent bottom crawlers are often presented whole. Don't be intimidated—jump right in and get messy.

– RAZOR CLAMS –

Large clams, often fried. A bit chewy, but the flavor is worth the jaw workout.

CHAPTER 9
HOW TO GET A SOUVENIR THAT LASTS FOREVER— A NORTHWEST TATTOO

1. Visit tattoo parlor with friend for courage.

2. Pick tattoo stencil off the wall.

3. Make sure tattooist uses new needle. Can you say "hepatitis"?

4. Bite leather strap to keep from screaming.

5. Watch vibrating needle chew a design into your flesh.

6. Put shirt (or if you were really brave, pants) back on.

7. Keep sterile salve/gauze on wound.

8. Wait about 10 days for scabs to fall off. That's when you'll learn if your tattooist was an artist or merely someone who couldn't find another job after release from prison.

9. Chart your aging process as you watch tattoo sag with time.

10. Years later, curse your selection of "Horny Devil" when trying to explain tattoo to your grandson.

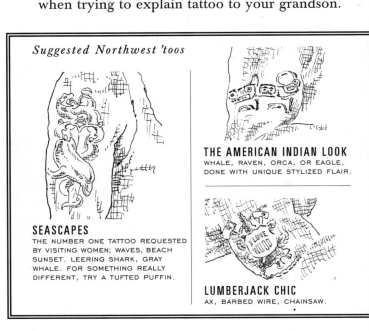

Suggested Northwest 'toos

SEASCAPES
THE NUMBER ONE TATTOO REQUESTED BY VISITING WOMEN; WAVES, BEACH SUNSET. LEERING SHARK, GRAY WHALE. FOR SOMETHING REALLY DIFFERENT, TRY A TUFTED PUFFIN.

THE AMERICAN INDIAN LOOK
WHALE, RAVEN, ORCA, OR EAGLE, DONE WITH UNIQUE STYLIZED FLAIR.

LUMBERJACK CHIC
AX, BARBED WIRE, CHAINSAW.

CHAPTER 10
H O W   T O
I N V E S T   I N   V I N Y L

The following albums must be added to your collection before you leave the Northwest:

1. *Electric Ladyland,* The Jimi Hendrix Experience
2. *The Fabulous Wailers at the Castle*
3. *The Kingsmen in Person*
4. *Pearl Jam, Seattle Washington Nov 6, 2000* (one of the multiple concert series released)
5. *Midnight Ride,* Paul Revere and the Raiders
6. *Ultramega OK,* Sound Garden
7. *Zoot Suit Riot,* Cherry Poppin' Daddies
8. *Songs of the Gray Whale*
9. *Who's Been Talkin,* Robert Cray Band
10. *Call the Doctor,* Sleater-Kinney
11. *Bleach,* Nirvana
12. *Here Are the Sonics*

CHAPTER 11
WHERE TO GRAB A SMOKE

1. Designated common spaces around arenas.
2. Rooftops of cinder-block buildings.
3. Bars with European names.
4. Open-air parks (but expect a severe thrashing if you throw your butt on the ground).

5. Designated smoking areas (these still exist in a total of seven restaurants).
6. Mall parking lots.
7. Campgrounds, but only while you are standing completely inside firepit.
8. Restrooms in highway rest areas.
9. Last row, third deck of every third stadium.
10. Cigar bars.

NOTICE: Most Northwesterners hate smoke—and smokers. In areas other than those listed above, smoking has usually been banned, and lighting up may result in a lengthy jail term (or at least a disapproving glare from a resident).

CHAPTER 12
SAMPLE NORTHWEST ADVENTURE:
CONQUER WHITE WATER IN A RAFT

Equipment checklist

- ❏ RIVER GUIDE (CHECK FOR LEATHERY SKIN, A SIGN OF EXPERIENCE)
- ❏ RAFT WITH RIGID FRAME
- ❏ PADDLE
- ❏ LIFE JACKET (THE HIGH-COLLAR, FULL-BODY KIND THAT HELPS KEEP YOUR HEAD UP)
- ❏ RAFTING SANDALS
- ❏ THROWABLE LIFESAVING DEVICE, WITH PLENTY OF ROPE
- ❏ QUICK-DRYING PANTS OR SHORTS
- ❏ T-SHIRT
- ❏ SUNGLASSES, WITH RETAINER
- ❏ SUNSCREEN
- ❏ HAT YOU WON'T MIND LOSING

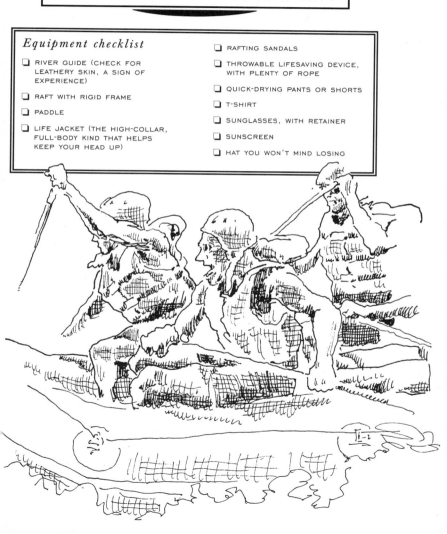

River-rafting know-how

1. As guide holds raft, climb in.
2. Ask which class of rapids you'll be encountering. (Class I or II = kind of like bike riding. Class IV or V = kind of like bull riding.)
3. Make sure cooler is filled with the right beer (Henry Weinhard's or Rainier, cans only).
4. Sit with body weight partly on side of raft and partly on inflated seat.
5. Wedge feet securely under the seat in front of you. Your feet are what holds you in the boat when things get bouncy.
6. Follow stroke instructions from your guide. Example: "Backpaddle. Backpaddle. OK. Stop. Stop! For the love of God, *stop!*"
7. If you can't hear guide's command over the thunder of the river, watch what the other paddlers are doing.
8. If you fall in, point feet downstream to absorb impact of the boulders.
9. For bragging rights back home, increase level of rapids you encountered by one. For example, if you tackled Class IV rapids on the Rogue River, say "Those Class V rapids were unbelievable."

CHAPTER 13
DEVELOP YOUR
TASTE FOR MICROBREWS

Proper brewpub behavior

1. Always order a pint. A 12-oz. glass of beer is an insult.

2. Don't hesitate to send a brew back. Kegs can go flat. Or sometimes a batch of beer just isn't what it should be.

3. Use a coaster.

4. Remember that pub food often means fatty food. Sure, there are exceptions such as McMenamins' grilled ahi tuna steak sand-wich with wasabi

mayo. But if you can't find anything low-fat on the menu, go for it—ask for a double order of home-made fries or some Walla-Walla sweet onion rings.

5. A brewpub isn't a drunks' bar. Brawls are consid-ered bad form.

6. Chat up your waiter/waitress. Good conversation may lead to free samples of other beverages.

7. Don't compare the pub's logo to something your nephew did in third-grade art class.

8. Don't bogart that barstool. If the pub is crowded and you're done sipping suds, kindly mingle and let a thirstier soul take your seat.

Microbrew terms

MICROBREW. Hand-crafted, quality beer brewed in small batches.

BREWPUB. A pub that serves beer brewed on the premises. Good examples are the McMenamins brewpubs found all over Oregon and Washington.

SAMPLER. A selection of 4-oz. taster glasses of microbrews served at a brewpub. A sampler plank at Rogue Brewing in Newport, Oregon, for example, might consist of Shakespeare Stout, Yellow Snow Pale Ale, Brutal Bitter, Dead Guy Ale, Imperial India Pale Ale, and Mocha Porter. The idea is to compare different microbrew styles.

HEAD. The wonderful creamy foam that tops your beer.

PINT. Big 16-oz. glass of your favorite brew. A few of the more generous brewpubs serve imperial pints—19 oz.

PORTER. A dark, sweet, malty style of beer.

STOUT. The heavy-tasting brew favored in Ireland.

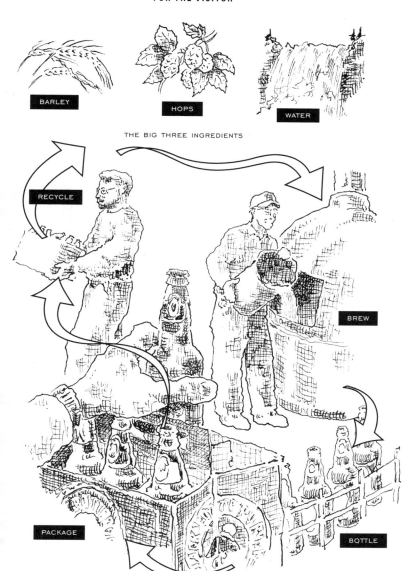

THE BIG THREE INGREDIENTS

BARLEY

HOPS

WATER

RECYCLE

BREW

PACKAGE

BOTTLE

*Beginner's guide to some perennial
Northwest favorites*

– DESCHUTES BLACK BUTTE PORTER –

Arguably ordered by more Northwest microbrew aficionados than
any other micro. Rich and malty.

– ROGUE'S SHAKESPEARE STOUT –

William himself would rise from the grave
for a pint of this robust beverage. An
ebony body yields a head that's pure and
creamy. Mellow chocolate aftertaste.

– GRANTS IMPERIAL PALE ALE –

This Washington IPA is characteristically pale
and refreshing, with that heavy hop aroma that
says you're a serious ale drinker.

– PYRAMID ESPRESSO STOUT –

Similar to motor oil in color, but thankfully not in taste.
Coffee-colored head, and a bit of coffee flavor as well as chocolate.

– WIDMER HEFEWEIZEN –

By law, this one should be served with with a slice
of lemon. An unfiltered wheat beer, cloudier than
Mount Rainier in springtime.

CHAPTER 14
NORTHWEST
BOOKSTORE PRIMER

---

1. Sell this book! Used bookstores abound in the region. After reading this book and your other vacation favorites, trade them in for something new to read on the way home.

2. On chilly mornings, seek out bookstore/coffee shop combos. To really feel like a local, read books about coffee while sipping it.

3. If guest author hails from the Northwest, ask them to sign multiple copies. Mail these unique gifts to those poor, unfortunate souls stuck back home.

4. Offer to check your backpack or shopping bag on the way in. Independent bookstores are often barely staying in business, and they fear shoplifters.

5. Leave your umbrella at the stand near the front door. Don't worry, there will be one.

6. Chat with the clerks about local authors and local topics. They'll have fascinating insights as to what's worth reading.

7. If you like the store, ask to be put on their mailing list. Many bookstores now have e-commerce or direct mail sales.

How to identify a first edition

First, look for the words "first edition." That's a pretty good clue. On the copyright page you'll often see a row of numbers: 1 2 3 4 5 6 7 8 9 10. One numeral gets deleted with each subsequent printing. Make sure the 1 appears; if not, it may not be a first edition. [Some publishers use a letter—Scribner's, for example, at one time used

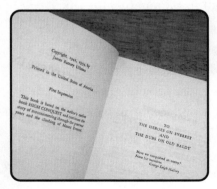

an "A."] Beyond these basic tips, hunting first editions gets complicated. But it will give you a reason to talk with the bookstore clerk. If you're not sure whether a hardcover book is a first edition, ask.

Dust jacket

Up to 40% of the value of a first edition will be in the dust jacket. One that's missing its dust jacket might seem like a real steal, but it's not.

CAUTION: If you visit Powell's, the world's largest bookstore, in Portland, Oregon, pick up a map on your way in. People have been lost in its aisles for days at a time. Search teams are expensive.

CHAPTER 15
READ THE
NORTHWEST CLASSICS

Top 10 can't-miss reads

1. *Sometimes a Great Notion.* 1963. Ken Kesey. Always a great novel, set in Oregon's timber country.

2. *The Left Hand of Darkness.* 1969. Ursula K. LeGuin. Arguably the finest, most inventive science fiction book ever written.

3. *The Natural.* 1952. Bernard Malamud. (Written during his teaching days at Oregon State University.) Think you don't like baseball? You'll like it after you read this.

4. *Dune.* 1965. Frank Herbert. Science fiction classic inspired by author's study of sand dunes on the Pacific Coast.

5. *The River Why.* 1983. David James Duncan. Great characters. Great fishing.

6. *Geek Love.* 1989. Katherine Dunn. The weirdest book ever written by this former Willamette Week columnist (or anyone else). You'll love it.

7. *Reservation Blues*. 1995. Sherman Alexie.
A crackling good read by a terrific
Native American author.

8. *Snow Falling on Cedars*. 1994. David Guterson.
Murder. Mystery. Puget Sound. The makings
of several late-night readings.

9. *Even Cowgirls Get the Blues*. 1976. Tom Robbins.
Former *Seattle Times* feature editor at his bizarre best.
Read the book, skip the movie.

10. *Undaunted Courage*. 1996. Stephen Ambrose.
It wasn't written in the Northwest, but with the
200th anniversary of Lewis and Clark's epic journey
being celebrated in 2005, it's a must
read. Besides, it's a great blueprint if
you want to retrace some of their
Northwestern steps.

CHAPTER 16
HOW TO APPRECIATE ANCIENT ROCK ART

Native American carvings and drawings, set in stone, have lasted centuries.

Pictographs are rock drawings.
Petroglyphs are rock carvings.

Visual key to petroglyphs

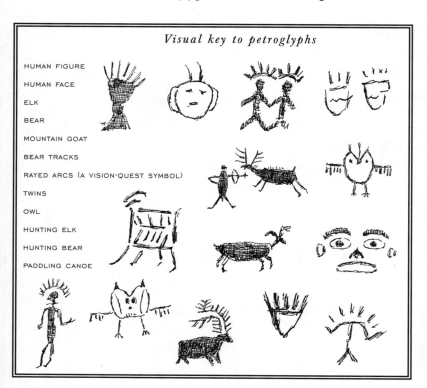

HUMAN FIGURE

HUMAN FACE

ELK

BEAR

MOUNTAIN GOAT

BEAR TRACKS

RAYED ARCS (A VISION-QUEST SYMBOL)

TWINS

OWL

HUNTING ELK

HUNTING BEAR

PADDLING CANOE

Sample deciphering of a series of pictographs

HUNTERS TRACK A BEAR BY ITS PRINTS AND
ENCOUNTER A MEDICINE MAN ON A VISION QUEST.

How to help preserve rock art

1. Don't touch any rock art.   **2.** Do not spray paint any rock faces.
3. Take a rubbing of a petroglyph (by laying tissue paper over it and rubbing with charcoal) only after asking permission from park ranger.
4. Report any vandalism to rock art sites.   **5.** Be glad you don't have to figure out a way to hang 300-pound slab of granite in your living room.

CHAPTER 17

WHAT TO DO IF YOU VISIT DURING HAY FEVER SEASON

You are visiting the allergy capital of the world. There is a veritable cornucopia of grasses, trees, and flowers here—all of them pumping out pollen. And mold spores are the other secret weapon of the ever-moist Northwest.

(**1**) Don't wait till it's too late. Spring hay fever season pounces like a hungry cougar. If you know you're vulnerable, start taking your medication several weeks in advance. (**2**) If you develop allergies after you arrive, consider an over-the-counter antihistamine. (**3**) If you're allergic to grass pollen, avoid the Willamette Valley in spring. (**4**) If you're allergic to the yellow pollen produced by many evergreens, April and May will be your enemies. (**5**) Make judicious use of eye drops. (**6**) The real benefit of a cold can is that it's cold. If you get caught unprepared for hay fever, gently roll an ice-cold beer over your eyeballs. It will temporarily relieve itching. Consume liquid for even more relief. (**7**) Consider a change of climate during your trip. You'll find a whole different ecosystem just a few hours' drive away. For example, many of the allergens present near the Cascades are almost absent on the coast. Or dry out your mucus membranes by heading across the Cascade Mountains to the arid interior. The only thing you're likely to be allergic to there are the gaudy patterns on the cowboy shirts.

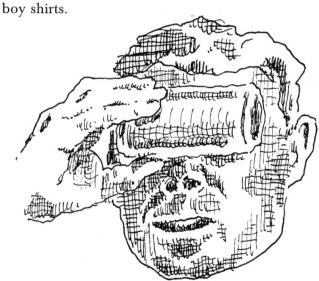

CHAPTER 18
HOW TO BE A SAVVY SPECTATOR AT A TIMBER CARNIVAL

Timber carnivals throughout the Northwest pit lumberjacks against each other in contests of power and speed.

What to look/listen for:

1. **THE EMCEE'S CADENCE WILL BE SOMETHING LIKE THIS:** "Timers ready? Contestants ready? 3, 2, 1, *chop!*"

2. **TREE CLIMBING.** Contestants make a timed run up a peeled tree using straps and spiked boots and rawboned muscle. First one to the top deserves a loud whistle.

AWE-INSPIRING NOTE: An agile lumberjack can climb a 100-foot pole in under 30 seconds.

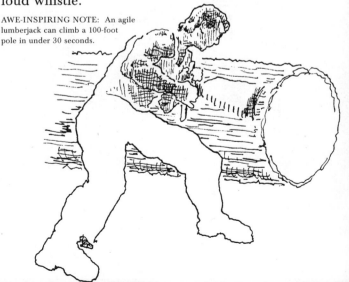

3. **TREE TOPPING.** Climbers each race up different poles, then cut off a section of the top. Hold your enthusiasm until the cut log hits the ground. That's when the timing ends.

4. **BIRLING.** A type of log rolling that gets personal. The objective is to spin one's opponent off the log. It takes incredible balance. Winner stays dry. Loser gets wet.

5. **AX THROWING.** Idea here is to show your appreciation that the ax is embedded in a target, not your skull.

6. **SAW BUCKING.** You might think it would require 250 pounds of muscle to cut through a two-foot-thick log like it was butter. Actually, technique is about 80% of the battle.

7. **STANDING CHOP EVENTS.** Here's your chance to see how axes really work. Lumberjacks cut through an 18-inch log faster than you could prune a small branch. When they miss, you'll know by the pitch of their yells whether they're wearing steel-toed boots.

How to throw an ax so it will stick in a target:

1. Raise double-bitted ax (that's one with two sharp edges) straight back overhead, making sure no one's behind you.
2. Aim for the center of the bull's-eye, which should be 60 inches from the ground.
3. Swing forward in exaggerated chopping motion.
4. Release the ax at 11 o'clock, slightly in front of you. Follow through with arms and legs.
5. Congratulate yourself on your newfound Paul Bunyanesque ability as ax sticks a bull's-eye.
6. If you try this at a competition and you should tie your opponent, there may be a sudden-death elimination format. Hopefully not your sudden death, but rather the end of the competition determined by the first thrower to stick a bull's-eye.

WARNING: Attempt only under supervision of a real lumberjack.

CHAPTER 19
JOURNEY TO THE
CENTER OF THE EARTH

(**1**) Always check in at the park or with guide before visiting a cave. (**2**) Many Northwest caves and lava tubes were formed by ancient volcanic eruptions, when lava forced its way through rock vents. (**3**) Lava tubes are a type of cave with relatively easy underground access. They are more for the "walk in and have a look around" style of curious caver versus the "rope up and descend into a black hell" style of adventurous spe-lunker. (**4**) Leave cave fish, legless lizards, blind snakes, rats, and other cave inhabitants undisturbed. This is a very fragile ecosystem. (**5**) Learn to distinguish bat guano from the mustard on your sandwich. (**6**) Do not step on any stalagmites. (These are the spires that grow from the cave floor. Stalactites are the ones that dangle from the ceiling.) (**7**) Leave a bread-crumb trail so you can find your way out.

Lava cave essentials

1. LANTERN
2. HEADLAMP
3. HIKING BOOTS
4. DISCUSSION WITH PARK RANGER
5. LAVA (PREFERABLY COLD, NOT HOT)
6. JACKET. MOST CAVES ARE AROUND 50°F YEAR-ROUND.
7. ANTI-BAT ALARM
8. ANTI-BAT GUANO (POOP TO THE UNINITIATED) HAT

NOTE: This step is necessary only when you're bringing kids—they'll love the fairy-tale aspect.

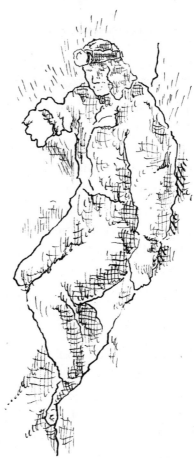

(**8**) If cave narrows, splits, or has precipitous dropoffs, turn back immediately.   (**9**) Do not try to use any exit other than the one where you entered.

CHAPTER 20
HOW TO AVOID ILLEGAL MARIJUANA PATCHES

Certain illicit drugs have been known to thrive in the Northwest's ultra-moist environment

(**1**) When hiking, avoid any area posted "No Trespassing," "No Outsiders," or "Touch my pot and die."

(**2**) When you pull into a farm to ask directions and are met by three Rottweilers, this is a good clue you are not welcome. (**3**) If you stumble upon marijuana plants, keep your cool. Back out slowly. (**4**) Do not trample the "crop." (**5**) Walk rapidly away from area. (**6**) Convince yourself the weeds are only being grown to manufacture legal hemp products. (**7**) Cross the area off as one of your "preferred hiking places" in your hiking guidebook. (**8**) Remember the location if you should ever develop any "medicinal" needs for the herb.

CHAPTER 21
HANDY TRICKS FOR BARTERING WITH HIPPIES AT AN OPEN-AIR FESTIVAL

1. Festivals flourish in the Northwest. Great values may be had on pots (and, occasionally, even pot), Native American handwork, blankets, batik, tie-dye shirts, worry stones, jewelry, sculptures, and other wares.

---

2. Quotes from the ancient languages:

I Dig you	I like you
Groovy	I can dig it
Far out	Extremely cool
Peace	Take it easy
Right on	Good job
Cool	Unchanged in 40 years

---

3. Recite passages from famous hippie-era writings. Ginsberg or Ferlinghetti poems. Timothy Leary. Jimi Hendrix songs. Tom Wolfe's *Electric Kool-Aid Acid Test* or Robert Pirsig's *Zen and the Art of Motorcycle Maintenance*.

4. Suggest that you're following the trail of the Magic Bus—it may get you a slight discount. (Ken Kesey led the Merry Pranksters on an odyssey through the Northwest in the mid-1960s.)

5. Cover your rental car with Grateful Dead stickers and say you're visiting past concert-site "shrines."

6. Acknowledge modern-day hippie-worthy bands: Phish, Widespread Panic.

7. Trade your day pack or sun cap for a lava lamp.

8. Consider the amount of handwork that went into a simple necklace before saying, "I think I've seen that at Wal-Mart."

9. When looking at gemstones in jewelry, examine with magnifying glass and then consult a small notebook. This will give you the air of an expert, even if you are not. Then utter, "it's on the cusp of quality I'll accept." Next, make a low-ball offer.

10. Remind the trader that asking for too much money is capitalistic; offer to help him/her seek a simpler lifestyle by paying 30% less.

CHAPTER 22
**WHAT TO DO WHEN YOU
ENCOUNTER STREET PEOPLE**

Tipping performers

1. Street creativity abounds. If a street musician pleases you, a fifty-cent or one-dollar tip is appropriate.

2. Same with other types of street artists. Creativity should be judged on costume and execution. Top Northwest street performers range from "the human rock," who is spray-painted to imitate granite and can remain motionless for hours, to a one-man band, complete with drums, guitar, harmonica, and your very own souvenir cassette for just $9.99.

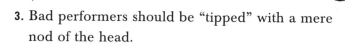

3. Bad performers should be "tipped" with a mere nod of the head.

How to handle a panhandler

1. Aggressive panhandlers should be ignored. Simply say "Sorry" and keep walking.

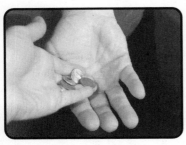

2. You may choose to tip friendly street people. Some always ask for the same amount, such as 13 cents or 35 cents. How they arrive at those numbers remains a mystery.

3. Panhandlers who appear to be a threat should be reported to police.

4. Inventive pleas deserve some coin. "I need some shampoo to prepare for my job interview" or "I just need a quarter more to get Tolstoy's *War and Peace*" are hard to ignore.

5. When in doubt, offer a banana. If someone is truly hungry, it is a welcome and inexpensive gesture.

CHAPTER 23
DEAL WITH DISASTER

How to survive a traffic jam

SCENARIO | You crest a hill, only to find eight miles of gridlock ahead.

(**1**) Do not abandon your vehicle, even when things seem hopeless. (**2**) Leave shortcuts to the locals. (**3**) Don't dislocate your neck trying to spot the cause of the backup. Northwest traffic jams defy logic. (**4**) Tune radio until NPR pours forth. (**5**) Laugh with the Car Guys. (**6**) Hope Car Guys will tell you what to do with your rapidly overheating radiator. (**7**) Photo opportunity: Check for visible mountains. (**8**) Strike up conversation with other travelers who've overheated and/or run out of gas.

(**9**) Borrow fellow strandee's cell phone to call AAA. Pull your hair out by the roots when you find your AAA bill in glove box, unpaid. (**10**) Next time, remember to put gallon jug of water in the trunk and fill gas tank before approaching Seattle or Portland.

What to do if you find yourself in a fog

SCENARIO | A fog rolls in so fast that you become enshrouded without warning.

ON THE BEACH (1) At first, the fog may appear to be nothing more than a light mist. It can roll in off the water in less than two minutes. (2) Observe how the 200 people that were on the beach with you have now disappeared. (3) Don't panic. After brief disorientation, make your way to your car. If you find yourself waist-deep in the ocean, you're going the wrong way.

ON A HIGHWAY (1) Slow your vehicle immediately (but don't jam on the brakes). Check your speedometer; fog makes it seem like you're moving slower than you are. (2) Turn on fog lights. High beams just reflect off the fog. (3) Back off quickly if you see brake lights ahead. (4) Use dangerous traffic condition as an excuse to pull into roadside outlet mall and kill a few hours shopping.

IN A RESIDENTIAL AREA (1) Abandon any hope of actually being able to read street names. (2) Use cell phone to call host and tell him or her you're lost. (3) Get busy signal. Hang up. Repeat as many times as necessary. (4) Park. Approach nearest front door to ask directions. (5) At appearance of large, hostile dog, retreat to car. (6) If fog doesn't lift, feel free to eat or drink the hostess gift you brought along.

How to handle a coffee-order mix-up

SCENARIO | You ordered a breve with almond flavor but received a breve with hazelnut syrup.

1. Sip the drink again, to make sure.

2. Once you're sure there's been a mistake, approach the barista. If there's a line, hold the beverage over your head and wave it gently back and forth.

   CAUTION: If the beverage is hot, wave your free hand.

3. Keep your eyes on the barista this whole time. Don't look at the other customers; they will sense something's amiss and move aside.

4. When the barista looks at you, say clearly: "Almond, not hazelnut." Baristas understand simple sentences.

5. The barista should remedy your problem before making any other customer's drink. If they do, a small additional tip is a nice gesture. If they make you wait, remove a quarter from their tip jar.

"Almond, not hazelnut"

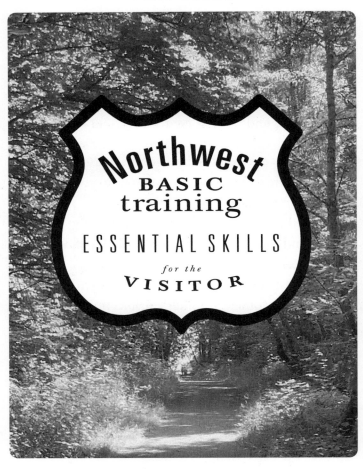

Awarded if you have completed
at least four of the following:

❑ Consumed minimum of two coffees daily.

❑ Returned from beach with shells and other natural objects you can name.

❑ Taken charge of ordering the wine at a seafood dinner.

❑ Found a wild huckleberry patch.

❑ Read *Snow Falling on Cedars*.

❑ Consumed filberts until sick.

❑ Found your way out of a fog.

❑ Ordered sampler plank in a brewpub and drank everything on it.

the umbrella

Oyster

& Clam

quilt

in the woods

SECTION No. 2	NEWCOMERS **A PRIMER**

There's no need to "ease into" the Northwestern lifestyle. As a resident, feel free to jump right in with both Nike-clad feet. The only thing formal here is the informality. Neckties must be surrendered at the border. "Old money" means wrinkled bills, not stuffed shirts. "Work hard, play hard" suddenly becomes a reality, not a cliché. You say goodbye to the sun, but also to skin cancer. The rain starts to roll right off your mossy back. In other words, you adapt. This section will help you fit in. And feel very comfortable very soon.

FIRST WEEK IN NORTHWEST:
❏ Wander into brewpub, commit faux pas by ordering Coors.
❏ Realize Pacific Time means three hours difference from 60% of America.
❏ Graciously accept free coffee cup from neighborhood coffee shop; mistakenly fill it with Folgers.
❏ Hang clothes outdoors to dry, assuming morning sun will last all day.

FIRST MONTH IN NORTHWEST:
❏ Move into loft, introduce yourself to four photographer neighbors.
❏ Add fleece items to your wardrobe.

❏ Unapologetically waste an entire Sunday morning lounging in bookstore.
❏ Explore Pacific beach, realizing why you added fleece to wardrobe.

FIRST YEAR IN NORTHWEST:
❏ Switch your second coffee order of the day to "tall skinny."
❏ Belly up to "your" bar stool at the brewpub most Fridays.
❏ Save $1,200 a year on gas by biking to work.
❏ Listen intently to a babbling brook.

CHAPTER 24
FINDING NORTHWEST LIVING SPACE

Basic Home Styles

1. HIPPIE DWELLING—TEEPEE, YURT, GEODESIC DOME. INEXPENSIVE, YIELDING ULTRA-SIMPLE LIFESTYLE. MAY OR MAY NOT INCLUDE RUNNING WATER. ELECTRICITY? WHO NEEDS IT?

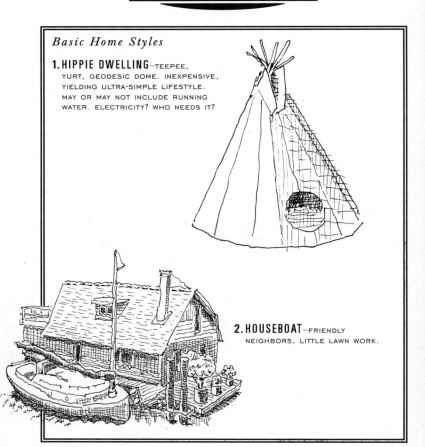

2. HOUSEBOAT—FRIENDLY NEIGHBORS, LITTLE LAWN WORK.

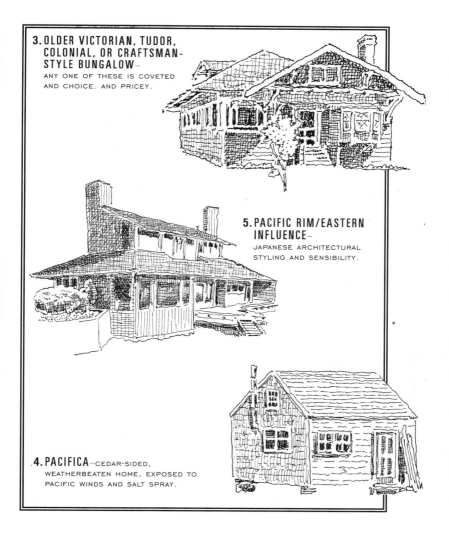

3. OLDER VICTORIAN, TUDOR, COLONIAL, OR CRAFTSMAN-STYLE BUNGALOW—
ANY ONE OF THESE IS COVETED AND CHOICE. AND PRICEY.

5. PACIFIC RIM/EASTERN INFLUENCE—
JAPANESE ARCHITECTURAL STYLING AND SENSIBILITY.

4. PACIFICA—CEDAR-SIDED, WEATHERBEATEN HOME, EXPOSED TO PACIFIC WINDS AND SALT SPRAY.

Things to look for

1. ROOF—Cedar is still the roof of choice. It's high-maintenance, it's flammable, and it can get brittle. But it sure looks cool.   **2. BASEMENT**—Builders figured out they didn't have to build basements, since they tend to fill with water, and tornadoes are scarce. Hence, basements are a bit scarce in the Northwest, but worth finding. Where else will you store all those driftwood sculptures you're going to carve one day? **3. LOTS OF LIGHT**—Northwest skies are often gloomy. Make sure your house isn't   **4. PLENTY OF NATIVE VEGETA-TION**—It looks good, and you'll save big time on your water bill.

Keys to becoming a good Northwest neighbor

(**1**) Always offer to water neighbors' lawn while they're on vacation. This is an easy promise to keep, since Mother Nature does your work for you.   (**2**) Compliment neighbors who landscape with Japanese bonsai plants. They have put in hundreds of hours of maintenance. Acknowledgment makes their day.   (**3**) Walk your dog with a promi-

NOTE: Extra neighborhood Brownie points for picking up other dogs' duty. Be sure to draw attention to yourself while carrying out this altruistic task by loudly announcing your actions: "I'm now picking up Mrs. Sander's dog's waste! I'm placing it in a bag. Just like I do every day."

nently displayed pooper-scooper and plastic baggie. Use them. (4) If your yard has fruit trees, pick fruit promptly when it's ripe. Rotting fruit attracts yellow-jackets. Test fruit for worms yourself. If you don't ingest anything white and wiggly, distribute to neighbors in recyclable brown paper bags.

CHAPTER 25
HOW TO BE A FACTOR IN NORTHWEST POLITICS: SIGNATURES, SIGNATURES, SIGNATURES

The Northwest is practically the birthplace of initiatives and referendums. And even though some say the initiative process has gotten way out of hand here, you can get into the swing of things simply by launching a bill of your own.

(1) Choose an issue you believe in. Examples: "We need a sales tax" (Oregon); "Our sales tax is too high" (Washington).   (2) Assemble your thoughts in a vaguely worded, rambling dissertation. Making the issue confusing is essential to getting it into the voter's pamphlet and onto the ballot.   (3) Choose a high-traffic area: downtown bus stop, sidewalk outside Starbucks, metered highway on-ramp at rush hour, porta-potties at a Huskies game.   (4) Thoroughly soak yourself so you'll appear miserable and cold. (5) Approach every potential signer with a lonely, pleading look. Make it clear you don't want money, just a signature.   (6) Make sure the person is a registered voter before you have them sign.   (7) Repeat steps 4, 5, and 6 tens of thousands of times.   (8) Submit

completed petition and signature sheets to state capitol by deadline.   (**9**) Pat yourself on the back as you envision how you're changing the system.   (**10**) On election night, watch your initiative get 112 votes.

```
CHAPTER 26
FIT IN:
START RUNNING
```

(1) The first task: Buy running shoes that fit your feet. Your ankle/foot may naturally roll in (pronation) or out (supination). The correct shoe will overcome either.   (2) Don't skimp. Shoes in the $50 range won't cut it. Look for full-foot air cushion or gel pad. (3) Eschew the big-box stores and try your neighborhood running shop instead. These typically offer lots of technical info and personal service. (You'll also pick up tips such as which running routes have the most mean dogs.)   (4) Once you've begun to run daily, buy a second pair of running shoes and alternate the pairs. This lets them dry out.   (5) All-natural fiber socks can bind up from sweat/heat and cause blisters. Look for a breathable blend of fibers that will transfer moisture.

Training Schedule

Go see your doctor. She'll probably say, "I can't believe it took you this long to start running." If you get a clean bill of health, stretch leg muscles. Then try this schedule:

ISN'T this a WALK dAY!

WEEK 1. WALK.
Good grief. Not another hill. Gasp.
15 minutes a day, 4 days.

WEEK 2. WALK.
God, my feet hurt. Not another dog. Ugh.
20 minutes a day, 5 days.

WEEK 3. WALK/RUN.
My side is killing me. Where are the Fritos?
30 minutes a day, 5 days.

WEEK 4. RUN.
The agony. I thought this was
supposed to be fun.
20 minutes a day, 4 days.

WEEK 5. RUN.
I'm throwing these shoes out.
25 minutes a day, 5 days.

WEEK 6. RUN.
Miss my run? Are you crazy?

CHAPTER 27
MASSAGE RELIEF
FOR ACHING FEET

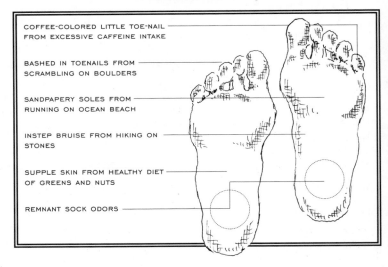

COFFEE-COLORED LITTLE TOE-NAIL
FROM EXCESSIVE CAFFEINE INTAKE

BASHED IN TOENAILS FROM
SCRAMBLING ON BOULDERS

SANDPAPERY SOLES FROM
RUNNING ON OCEAN BEACH

INSTEP BRUISE FROM HIKING ON
STONES

SUPPLE SKIN FROM HEALTHY DIET
OF GREENS AND NUTS

REMNANT SOCK ODORS

1. Find willing partner by offering to trade massages.

2. Have partner lie on his or her stomach.

3. Rub some massage oil into your hands.

4. Apply thumb pressure to the sole of the foot, stroking from heel to toe. Use gentle thumb pressure to work the heel area.

5. Have partner turn face up.

6. Make a loose fist and rub/rotate it

into the instep. This area deserves plenty of work, as it may be the source of foot pain.

7. End by "milking" or pulling on the foot. Start at heel, grasping foot with both hands, then milk by pulling hands toward toes. Gently pull and massage each toe.

8. Trade places.

Saying observed on wall of University of Oregon training room:

"The antidote for stress is running. The antidote for running is a good foot massage."

CHAPTER 28
SURVIVE THE REI SPRING SALE

Preparation

(**1**) Practice deep knee bends for stooping to bottom shelves. (**2**) Run a reconnaissance mission. Map out areas you want to hit on sale day. (**3**) Practice throwing elbows to clear crazed shoppers away from your targeted merchandise. (**4**) Arrive the night before to get front-of-line position. Curl up under blanket in lawn chair.

Sale day

1. VISIT BACKPACK SECTION FIRST—This strategy allows you to stuff in your subsequent purchases and carry them on your back. **2. NEXT, GPS SYSTEMS AND COMPASSES**—In case you lose your way in the massive Seattle store or

want to find a different REI location, you can punch in your coordinates and let a satellite guide you. **3. ON TO PARKAS**—Always a mad rush to see if there are any discounted waterproof breathable parkas. **4. GRAB A**

BITE—Time for a food break: Oberto turkey jerky. Be sure to pay after scarfing it down. **5. NEW SHOES AND SOCKS**—As your feet start to hurt, get some fresh socks. Then hiking boots to continue your journey. **6. HEAD FOR CLIMBING GEAR**—If you're among the one-half of one percent who have the guts and fitness to climb rock, buy a bunch of climbing gear. Even if you don't climb, the harness, pitons, rope, etc. will look cool in your closet, or scattered casually around your living room. **7. TAKE EXERCISE BREAK**—If you're at the Seattle store, approach the climbing peak. About 25 feet up, your arms will turn to jelly and your legs will start shaking in an embarrassing manner. Don't worry. If you fall, the rope and harness will snap you back to reality. **8. SEEK FIRST AID IF NECESSARY**—To treat the various bruises, nicks, and contusions you picked up on the rock face, head to the portable Adventure Medical first-aid kits.

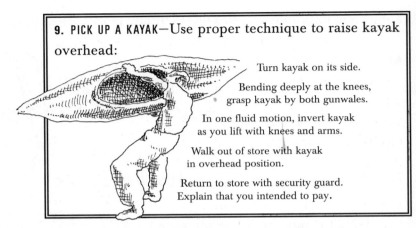

9. PICK UP A KAYAK—Use proper technique to raise kayak overhead:

Turn kayak on its side.

Bending deeply at the knees, grasp kayak by both gunwales.

In one fluid motion, invert kayak as you lift with knees and arms.

Walk out of store with kayak in overhead position.

Return to store with security guard. Explain that you intended to pay.

10. FINISH UP AT SLEEPING BAGS—Obviously time for a nap. Thanks to the store's climate-controlled environment, a bag rated +35°F will suffice.

CHAPTER 29
**TAKE TIME FOR
A DAY HIKE**

Clothing

(**1**) Supportive hiking boots. Make sure they're broken in to prevent blisters. Stout enough to prevent ankle sprains. Light enough to prevent exhaustion.
(**2**) Socks. Wool/micro-fiber combination to wick sweat away.   (**3**) Hiking shorts with at least 20 pockets.

Don't worry about finding uses for all of them—looking good is considered function enough. (**4**) Layers for torso. T-shirt. Fleece, if morning is cold. Light windbreaker. (**5**) Sun-thwarting hat.

What to put in your day pack

IDEAL DAY PACK, NAMED CAMELBAK, COMES WITH ITS OWN BUILT-IN WATER RESERVOIR

RAIN JACKET

FIRST-AID KIT

GORP. MAKE YOUR OWN: ½ PART CAROB CHUNKS, 1 PART RAISINS, 1 PART DRIED APRICOTS, 5 PARTS PEANUTS/CASHEWS

LUNCH. FOODS THAT WON'T SPOIL OR SQUISH

TOPO MAP AND FOREST SERVICE TRAIL PASSES

COMPASS

ON-FOOT HIKING JOURNAL

SPACE BLANKET (FOR EMERGENCY SHELTER, WARMTH, OR REFLECTOR IF LOST)

CORD/ROPE

SMALL CAMERA

GERBER MULTI-PLIER TOOL. CONTAINS KNIVES, PLIERS, SCREWDRIVERS, FILE, SAW, KITCHEN SINK

WHISTLE

What to do when you get lost

1. Stay put. The people who know where you went will come looking for you.

2. Blow three blasts from the whistle every 15 minutes.

3. Erect emergency shelter with space blanket.

Run 6-foot cord from one tree fork to another, 3 feet off ground.

Fold 12 inches of space blanket over cord, drape excess to windward side. Trap a rock in each corner of blanket (or use grommets, if provided).

Cut four stakes.

Stake four corners to ground. The high side of the shelter will have longcords. The low side will be on the ground.

Hike the forest, then eat it

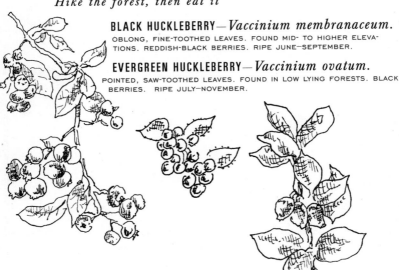

BLACK HUCKLEBERRY—*Vaccinium membranaceum.*
OBLONG, FINE-TOOTHED LEAVES. FOUND MID- TO HIGHER ELEVATIONS. REDDISH-BLACK BERRIES. RIPE JUNE—SEPTEMBER.

EVERGREEN HUCKLEBERRY—*Vaccinium ovatum.*
POINTED, SAW-TOOTHED LEAVES. FOUND IN LOW LYING FORESTS. BLACK BERRIES. RIPE JULY—NOVEMBER.

RED HUCKLEBERRY—*Vaccinium parvifolium.*
FOUND SCATTERED OVER BROAD AREAS WEST OF CASCADE CREST. BRIGHT RED BERRIES. RIPE JULY—SEPTEMBER.

WOODLAND STRAWBERRY—*Fragaria vesca.*
SAWTOOTHED LEAVES ON HAIRY STALKS. FOUND IN LOWLANDS, CLEARINGS, FOREST TRAILS. RED BERRIES. RIPE JUNE—AUGUST.

TRAILING BLACKBERRY—*Rubus ursinus.*
COMPOUND, TOOTHED LEAVES IN THREES. LOGGED AREAS, OPEN FORESTS, MEADOWS. REDDISH/BLACK BERRIES. RIPE JULY—AUGUST.

HIMALAYAN BLACKBERRY—*Rubus procerus.*
LARGE, BROAD LEAVES. STOUT CANES WITH FLESH-TEARING THORNS. ROADSIDES, CLEAR CUT AREAS. RIPE JULY—OCTOBER.

SALMONBERRY—*Rubus spectabilis.*
LARGE LEAVES, CANED SHRUB. A TASTY TREAT IN CREEK BOTTOMS, SWAMPS, OR OTHER WET COASTAL AREAS. RED BERRIES. RIPE LATE JUNE—AUGUST.

CHAPTER 30

SKILLS FOR THE ROOKIE CAMPER

How to light a propane lantern

1. Remove lantern top, or open door, depending on style you have.
2. Tie on mantle(s).
3. Light mantle with match.
4. Once mantle is burning, shut door or replace dome.
5. Turn on gas.
6. Light in designated area with match.

Pitching a typical dome tent by lantern light

Murphy's Law states that all camping trips will be prone to departure delays, necessitating setting up camp at twilight:

(1) Remove very expensive tent from stuff bag (realizing you will never again be able to fit it inside that bleeping little bag).
(2) Separate poles. Don't cut the bungee cord connecting them. That's supposed to be there. (3) Place tarp on ground where tent will go. If you missed removing any

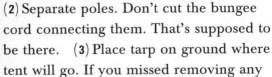

rocks from area, you will know it about 3 AM.   (**4**) Spread tent out. It helps if slots for poles are facing up.   (**5**) Stake the four corners of the tent.   (**6**) Typically, tent will feature some slots, plastic clips, or notches for poles. Slide assembled poles through appropriate spots.   (**7**) Anchoring one end of pole, raise the tent by bowing poles. (**8**) Slide other pole through slots and cross first pole, forming an X.   (**9**) Pull side gussets tight, and stake to ground. (**10**) Done. Check watch. If less than half an hour has elapsed, celebrate with some filtered water. If more than six hours have passed, consider a Winnebago.

Build a fire in wet conditions

(**1**) Choose area with a large boulder, hill, or log as partial windbreak. Do not build fire under overhanging branches. If they're wet or snow-laden, they'll bomb your fire with moisture.   (**2**) Use ax to re-split wet logs and expose dry surfaces. Or gather dead wood that's been protected.   (**3**) Dig a shallow fire pit, removing wet leaves, wet pinecones, or wet earth. (**4**) Use your pocketknife to make "fuzz sticks"—cut curls down sides of kindling sticks, giving fire more surface to grab and more oxygen. (**5**) Make a pyramid fire base. Basically, use four split logs to form a square. (**6**) Teepee up kindling in middle, with tinder or dry paper at its core (in an emergency use the front two pages and the back page of this book).

(**7**) Strike your waterproof matches and ignite (you can waterproof wooden matches by dipping them in paraffin wax).

(**8**) Keep enough fuel on the fire and it will take a monsoon to put it out. (**9**) Dry yourself off. Ignite a few marshmallows into fireballs. Make some coffee. Maybe a little rain isn't so bad after all.

CHAPTER 31
**LIVE-TRAP
YOUR NEIGHBORS**

PROBLEM | You've found a nice place to live that backs up to a spectacular forest—and its four-legged bandits, the raccoon and the opossum.

1. Obtain positive ID of problem creature (you don't want to tackle skunks or coyotes). Sprinkle baby powder under vents where critter may be entering house, or along night paths. Check footprints in morning. Compare to chart.

2. Locate traps between trees in areas known to be frequented by 'coons.

3. Bait trap with marshmallows and grapes. This will discourage neighborhood cats, yet appeal to night prowlers' taste for sweets.

4. Check your trap every morning. Look closely. Even the biggest raccoon blends into its surroundings very well.

5. If trap is full, remove.

   WARNING: Animal will be angry. Never handle the live trap without wearing heavy leather gloves.

6. Check with local authorities on where you may take the animal. However, if you've caught a neighbor's Schnauzer, discreetly return it without contacting authorities.

7. CAUTION: Wild animals stink! Never place in enclosed automobile. If you don't have a pickup, borrow one.

8. Drive to a remote state park area. After obtaining permission from park ranger, release critter to bother unknown picnickers.

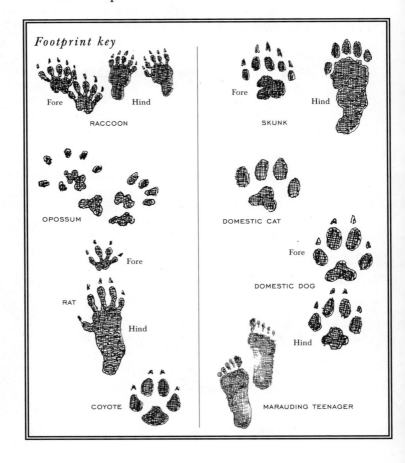

Footprint key

RACCOON — Fore, Hind

SKUNK — Fore, Hind

OPOSSUM

DOMESTIC CAT

RAT — Fore, Hind

DOMESTIC DOG — Fore, Hind

COYOTE

MARAUDING TEENAGER

Pest deterrent options:

(1) Sprinkle hot peppers around garden. (2) Wear a T-shirt for three days. Leave in garden. It will keep raccoons (and everything else) away. (3) Encourage your dog to perform his daily duty in area where raccoons have been a problem. (4) For moles, rats, or mice, the oldest method is still the best: Get a cat. (5) In places where pests are actively feeding, crumble granny's fruit cake and spread over area. Pests will not return for a second helping. (6) If raccoons are nesting in your yard, dial your battery-operated radio to heavy metal. Leave it on all night. The mother raccoon will move her young to a more ear-friendly site.

CHAPTER 32
HOW TO CUT YOUR OWN CHRISTMAS TREE IN THE WILD

---

(1) Check with the U.S. Forest Service for public lands where tree cutting is allowed. (2) Measure height of your ceiling. A 14-foot tree means either vaulted ceilings or patching the

sheetrock.   (**3**) Gather relatives and drive to convenient area.   (**4**) Compare the advantages of various trees.   (**5**) Make your final selection.   (**6**) After asking your relatives to stand back, saw tree off at ground level. This way you won't leave a tripping hazard. (**7**) Yell "Timber!" with great gusto.   (**8**) Drag tree to car. Realize you forgot to bring bungee cords. Improvise: Lash tree to your roof rack with shoelaces.   (**9**) At home, unload tree. Stand it upright on your driveway. Now bounce it up and down exactly 27 times and spin it around as though it were a dance partner. This will get rid of the spiders and dead needles.

Types of Chrismas trees

DOUGLAS FIR. PSEUDOTSUGA MENZIESII.
NEEDLES 1¼". RED-BROWN BARK DISTINCTIVE WITH ITS
DEEP FURROWS.

GRAND FIR. ABIES GRANDIS. NEEDLES FLAT, 1½", WITH
WHITE STRIPE ON UNDERSIDE. GRAY-BROWN BARK IS ALMOST
SMOOTH OR LIGHTLY FURROWED.

NOBLE FIR. ABIES PROCERA. NEEDLES FLAT, 1¼", BLUE-GREEN, FRAGRANT. DIS-
TINCTIVE NEEDLE PATTERN: THEY GROW IN PERFECT CYLINDER AROUND BRANCHES.
GRAYISH TO REDDISH-BROWN BARK, TYPICALLY SMOOTH.

CHAPTER 33
**HOW TO AVOID MOWING
YOUR LAWN**

PROBLEM | Northwest lawns can grow up to three inches per week.

Fight back

ANTI-MOWING STRATEGY #1 –Eliminate all grass. Cover lawn area with bark.

ANTI-MOWING STRATEGY #2 –Cover lawn area with attractive pine needles (now fetching premium dollars in California).

ANTI-MOWING STRATEGY #3 –
Let nature take its course. Allow moss to take over your lawn. Remember: Moss is green, grass is green. Moss fills in the bare spots nicely.

How to make moss your friend

(**1**) Learn how to decorate with moss. Make Martha jealous. Create moss centerpieces, moss coasters, moss candlesticks. (**2**) Moss makes an attractive covering for landscape boulders. (**3**) Moss can make a dead tree look alive. (**4**) Moss makes a relatively nonflammable coating for your roof. (**5**) Moss may be used to pack gaping wounds. (**6**) Very wet moss takes the sting out of bee stings. (**7**) Moss makes a great cushion for backyard games of football or volleyball. (**8**) A handful of moss acts as an excellent dustcloth.

CHAPTER 34
**H O W   T O   B E   A
M I C R O B R E W   M A S T E R**

Brew enthusiast's glossary

LAGER—Aka plain old beer. Not usually a microbrew. The yeast determines the difference between a lager and an ale. Lagers are bottom fermented, with the yeast working at the bottom of the brew.

ALE—Generally speaking, the wonderful complex flavors best experienced in brewpubs are the work of the ale family. Ales may be sweet or fruity or very strong. Ales are top fermented.

PALE ALE—Ranges in color from honey gold to coppery red. These ales are very hoppy and more bitter than most ales. They tend to utilize the Cascade hops of this region to their fullest extent. Pale ales with a bit of a floral aroma and just a hint of a spicy finish top the list.

INDIA PALE ALE (IPA)—Even hoppier than regular pale ale. Is it more bitter or just bigger on flavor? You'll have to decide for yourself. The name comes from British ales brewed to survive the voyage to India in the late 18th century. The higher hop content tends to preserve the product. Beware: IPAs also have a higher alcohol content.

WHEAT ALE—A wonderful Northwest invention by Hart Brewing Company in Kalama, Washington, and a cloudier version perfected by the Widmer brothers called Hefeweizen. Lemon wedge completes a wheat ale.

BITTER—Normally a negative, the term "bitter" in regard to beer merely refers to the edge of the hop bite. A good bitter will be smooth and pleasant. Bitter needs to be drawn from the tap to be appreciated.

PORTER—A sweet, malty, dark brew that's a favorite up and down the Northwest coast. This product gives the malt flavors a chance to shine. "Rich" is the word that comes to mind. Deschutes Brewing's Black Butte Porter has the dark color, rich flavor, and balance of hops and malt that have made all the microbrew porters popular.

STOUT—The blackest of ales, "stoutest" of brews. Robust and full-bodied, it has flavors that may be described as coffeelike, and indeed, some stouts are made with coffee. The distinctive head is creamy and a rich tan color. Hoppy aroma. Should be served fairly warm, 55° to 60°. Russian or imperial stout is the hoppiest, most brutal of beers, up to 10.5% alcohol by volume.

Pour the ultimate glass of beer

1. First, smash all your 12-ounce beer glasses. From now on you will use only pints. Typically, a pint glass widens at the top, making it ideal for a tap pour.

2. Tilt the glass or mug at a 30-degree angle.

3. Begin your pour down the side, adjusting the angle as necessary based on the beer's foaminess.

4. Is it a rapid foamer? Angle the glass even more.

5. Your result should be two and a half or three fingers of foam, or head.

6. Like a wine connoisseur, take this opportunity to sniff the beer's bouquet.

7. The first few sips of beer and foam teach you the beer's taste. Is it a bit nutty? Do you taste a hint of chocolate or coffee? Is it a "hoppy," intense flavor?

CHAPTER 35
FORM YOUR OWN NORTHWEST GARAGE BAND

Checklist

❑ DRUMS

5-PIECE DRUM SET

CRASH AND RIDE CYMBAL

HIGH HAT

DOUBLE BASS PEDAL

❑ GUITARS

BASS: FOUR- OR FIVE-STRING

ACOUSTIC: THE MORE SOLID WOOD THE BETTER. TAYLOR, TAKAMINE, YAMAHA

ELECTRIC: FENDER

❑ ATTITUDE

PART SURLY, PART ENERGY, PART FUN

❑ AMPS

GUITAR AMP, MINIMUM WATTAGE: TUBE 40 WATTS, OR TRANSISTOR 80 WATTS

BASS AMP, MINIMUM WATTAGE: 250 WATTS

❑ PUBLIC ADDRESS (PA)

SPEAKERS: 15-INCH WITH HIGH-FREQUENCY HORNS AND SPEAKER STANDS

MONITORS: TWO

MIXER: POWERED MIXER WITH INPUTS FOR ALL GUITARS

MIKES: ONE FOR EACH PERSON WHO'S GOING TO SING, HARMONIZE, OR GRUNT

Basic chord progression

Repeat fifty times.
Add lyrics no one can
understand. You've got
the makings of a song.

(For aching fingers, see page 156.)

uHH
looE
Loo-i
Ohh
ohH...

CHAPTER 36
GOLF IN THE RAIN.
OR DON'T GOLF AT ALL.

Dress for it

WATERPROOF SHOES—If your feet are soaked after the second hole, you still have 4½ hours of misery ahead.

LIGHTWEIGHT, WATERPROOF, BREATHABLE JACKET—Emphasis on "breathable."

UMBRELLA—On the golf course, you're either walking, hitting, or standing around. The umbrella's for the standing-around part.

Golf tips

(**1**) Just because it's wet doesn't mean you can't be competitive. (**2**) Heavy air and wet greens are a consideration. You won't hit as long from the tee or off the fairway under those conditions. (**3**) The best strategy is to hit the fairway rather than try for an extra 20 yards on your drive. (**4**) When fairways are wet, the rough will be even wetter. Remember, you score with your short game. (**5**) The greens hold your ball much better when wet. A ball hit onto a wet green won't roll for 15 yards. (**6**) Because the green will hold the ball better, you can go for the pin. (**7**) Remember, the ball won't break, or react to dips on the green, as much when greens are wet as when they are dry.   (**8**) Increased speed is everything when you're putting in wet conditions.   (**9**) Spend some extra time on the putting green before you tee off. (**10**) Blame your 30-over-par score on "the *&%$#@@# weather!"   (**11**) Take extra care cleaning clubs after playing in wet conditions.

Use nylon brush to clean woods.

Use wire brush to clean irons.

Dry clubs carefully before putting them away.

CHAPTER 37
**HOW TO
SHUCK AN OYSTER**

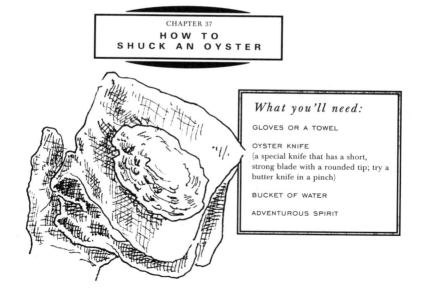

What you'll need:

GLOVES OR A TOWEL

OYSTER KNIFE
(a special knife that has a short, strong blade with a rounded tip; try a butter knife in a pinch)

BUCKET OF WATER

ADVENTUROUS SPIRIT

Dig out

(**1**) Hold the oyster
with the cupped
side down and
the hinged side
away from you.

NOTE: To avoid skewering your hand, wear heavy
gloves, or trap the oyster (cupped side
down) on a cutting board with a heavy towel.

(**2**) Find a place along the front edge where you can
begin wedging in the knife. Some shuckers like to
break a bit off the front shell with pliers. (**3**) Start
wedging the knife in, wiggling and cajoling it to separate the shells a bit. (Shells
crack and break off easily.
You may need several
attempts.) (**4**) Once you can
get the tip of the knife
between the shells, tilt the
handle up and separate the
adductor muscle from the bottom
shell by sliding the knife blade
downward. (**5**) Rinse off the meat and replace the
shucked oyster in one half of the shell.

Dig in

Down the hatch. Raw. Just swallow 'em whole! If you can avoid gagging on the slick texture, chew to release the flavors. This is an acquired taste.

CAUTION: Be sure oysters have been kept on ice, and are alive with shells closed. Oysters, like other raw shellfish, occasionally contain parasites. Consider it a small risk for a tasty reward.

FOR THE TIMID | Pan-fried oysters

If you don't have the stomach for raw oysters, fry 'em.

1. Coat with cornmeal.
2. Pour canola oil into heavy skillet until it's deep enough to come halfway up an oyster and heat to medium.
3. Brown oyster on one side. Flip.
   Cooking time: about a minute or a minute and a half.

CHAPTER 38

A BRIEF HISTORY
OF NORTHWEST FOOTWEAR

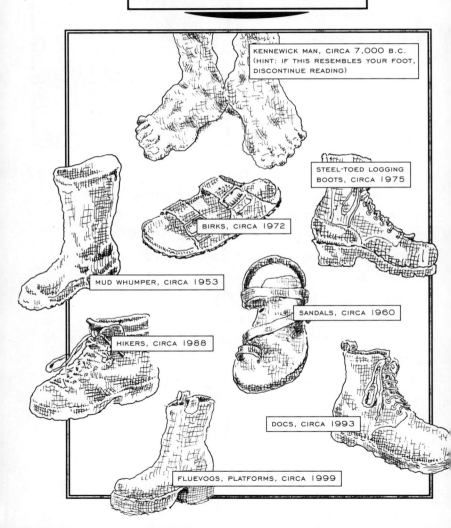

KENNEWICK MAN, CIRCA 7,000 B.C.
(HINT: IF THIS RESEMBLES YOUR FOOT,
DISCONTINUE READING)

STEEL-TOED LOGGING
BOOTS, CIRCA 1975

BIRKS, CIRCA 1972

MUD WHUMPER, CIRCA 1953

SANDALS, CIRCA 1960

HIKERS, CIRCA 1988

DOCS, CIRCA 1993

FLUEVOGS, PLATFORMS, CIRCA 1999

CHAPTER 39
DEALING WITH NORTHWEST CLAY AND SAND

Salvaging clay-stained clothes

(**1**) Soak clothes in precleaner. (**2**) Wash with detergent (one that contains bleach if they're white). (**3**) If first round of washing doesn't work, try again before drying. (**4**) Still red stained? It was a shirt, now it's a rag.

Assault on hardened clay

Clay here in the Northwest is a bit like those chunks of ice that build up between tires and mudflaps in the Midwest—once it hardens, Rodin could carve sculptures out of it. Nothing's worse to clean off your shoes than hardened clay. (Well, there is something worse to clean off your shoes. But that's another story.)

(**1**) Chip it off with hammer and chisel, just like concrete. (**2**) Or soak, soak, soak. Soak the soles of the shoes in a solution of mild detergent and water. Hose it off immediately before it dries again. (**3**) If all else fails, get out your jackhammer. Clay dries to the consistency of aged concrete. Good luck.

Got a beach cabin? Build this shoe cleaner

The world's simplest sand scraper should be a must at every beach cabin up and down the Pacific.

(1) Choose a spot convenient to the cabin entry, but out of the way so people won't trip over your shoe cleaner.   (2) Using 2-inch, 5-penny nails, nail a hard-bristled wooden brush to the deck or porch floor. (3) Take two other brushes and, using heavy-duty scissors, trim bristles to ¾" long. Now nail them at right angles to the sides of the first brush so they form a square letter "U."   (4) Stand back and admire your own cleverness.

CHAPTER 40
**HOW TO
SPLIT WOOD**

Procedure

(1) Put on goggles.   (2) Saw your fresh-cut wood into 18-inch logs.   (3) Set the log on tree stump or other chopping block.   (4) Use a

maul to split large logs—7 inches to 15 inches in diameter. (5) Use an ax for smaller logs. (6) Swing ax over one shoulder, pulling it rapidly down while aiming for center of log.

CAUTION: If you value your toes, don't get distracted.

(7) Smile with satisfaction as log splits cleanly with a loud crack. (8) Stack your wood under cover, away from the house. (9) Season six months.

Sharpen your ax

1. Now that you've dulled your ax, sharpen it.
2. Clamp ax head in vise clamp, sharp side up.
3. Lay medium-cut file flat against blade, draw it up.
4. Alternate strokes on each side of ax head.
5. Oil to prevent rust.
6. Put away in sheath.

> ### Types of firewood
>
> **ALDER**
> AN IDEAL CHOICE. MOST COMMON NORTHWEST FIREWOOD.
>
> **OAK**
> VERY HARD, BURNS SLOWLY. DIFFICULT TO SPLIT.
>
> **WALNUT**
> A GOOD HARDWOOD FOR FIRES.
>
> **MAPLE**
> GOOD CHOICE. SPLITS EASILY.
>
> **DOUGLAS FIR, PINE**
> CONTAINS TOO MUCH PITCH AND CREATES EXCESS CREOSOTE.

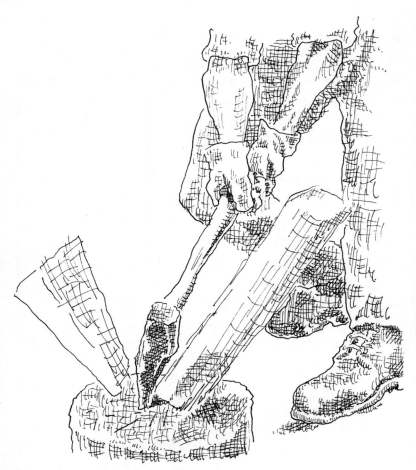

WARNING: Wear gloves around the woodpile. Woodpiles are one of the places frequented by the nastiest spider west of the Cascades: the Hobo spider, *Tegenaria agrestis*. Also known as the aggressive house spider, this large, brown spider is likely to attack when a giant hand picks up its firewood home. The bite causes a red welt up to 15 cm in diameter, which blisters in a day. Tissue loss may occur, and scarring. Migraine headache, nausea, and weakness may develop. Though not life threatening, Hobo bites should be treated by a doctor.

CHAPTER 41
**NORTHWEST BACKYARD
BIRDING BASICS**

Specs on your bird-watching specs:

BRAND—Windriver or Bushnell

FIELD OF VIEW—300' to 450' (this means the width of the area you see through binoculars at 1000 meters)

OPTICS—8 x 30 great, 7 x 25 adequate

OPTICS NOTE | First number is the magnification; second number is the size of objective lens—larger number allows more light to enter for better viewing.

Native plants birds really like

TREES—Western red cedar, vine maple, red alder, crabapple

SHRUB—Redflowering currant, Oregon grape, juniper, cotoneaster

Backyard species that make
interesting neighbors

PILEATED WOODPECKER

<u>PICOIDES ARCTICUS.</u> 16".
POINTED, FLAMING RED CREST,
BLACK BODY FEATHERS. LIVES
IN DEAD TREES, GIVING YOU
AN EXCELLENT EXCUSE NOT TO
PAY FOR TREE REMOVAL.
"WICKA-WICKA-WICKA" CALL.

WESTERN BLUEBIRD

<u>SIALIA MEXICANA.</u> 7".
BRILLIANT BLUE COLOR.
FEMALE HAS GRAY HEAD,
ORANGISH BREAST. A RARE
SIGHT IN SUBURBIA. NOT
TO BE CONFUSED WITH LARGER
BLUEJAY. SONG: SOUNDS
A BIT LIKE "CHEER, CHEER-LIE."

CEDAR WAXWING

<u>BOMBYCILLA GARRULUS.</u> 7".
BEAUTIFUL BLEND OF BROWNS,
GRAYS, AND YELLOWS.
YELLOW BAND AT END OF
GRAY TAIL. CALL SOUNDS
LIKE "CEE-CEE-CEE."

NORTHERN FLICKER

<u>COLAPTES AURATUS.</u> 12".
MALE FLICKER HAS THICK,
RED MUSTACHE-LIKE FEATHERS
BESIDE ITS THROAT. (LUCKILY,
FEMALE LACKS MUSTACHE,
AS THERE ARE NO WOODPECKER
DEPILATORY PRODUCTS ON
THE MARKET.) SONG SOUNDS
LIKE "FLICK-ER," HENCE
THE NAME.

MOURNING DOVE

<u>ZENAIDA MACROURA.</u> 10".
GRACEFUL, ELEGANT GRAY/TAN
COLORING. SMALL HEAD,
LONG TAIL. SONG: VERY
SOOTHING "COO-COO-COO."

SPOTTED TOWHEE

<u>PIPILO MACULATUS.</u> 7"-8".
BACK AND WINGS BLACK
WITH WHITE SPOTS. TIP
OF TAIL WHITE. RED EYES.
SONG: DRAWN OUT "MEEEEE."

SONG SPARROW

<u>MELOSPIZA MELODIA.</u> 6".
HANDSOME RUST COLOR
WITH LIGHTER GRAY
STRIPING. SONG: GREAT
SONGSTER, LISTEN FOR
THE "ZEE ZEE DID DEE."

CHAPTER 42
LANDLUBBER'S GUIDE TO SEAFOOD

Choosing fresh fish

(**1**) Buy salmon from American Indians as they catch it.   (**2**) When buying whole fish, check that the gills (if present) are bright red.   (**3**) Look for clear eyes. They're the window to tasty flesh.   (**4**) Make sure the skin is resilient; when poked, the flesh should spring back.   (**5**) The fish should smell fresh, not unpleasantly "fishy," and there should be no ammonia smell.   (**6**) There should be no brown discoloration or darkened edges.

Choosing shellfish

(**1**) Make sure they are alive. For clams and mussels, the shells should be closed or should close when touched.   (**2**) Make sure they are on ice.   (**3**) Look for foaming coming out of shells (not good).

How to gut a trout

(**1**) Take one whole trout. Make a deep cut, right behind the jaw, from bottom to top of head.   (**2**) Turn the fish upside down and cut all the way along the belly starting at the anus, making sure to cut away from the hand holding the fish. (**3**) Grasp the gills and front fins. Pull. Gills, fins, and guts all come out in one yank. (**4**) Press your thumb along the inside of the backbone and strip out the dark kidneys and blood. (**5**) Rinse. Done.

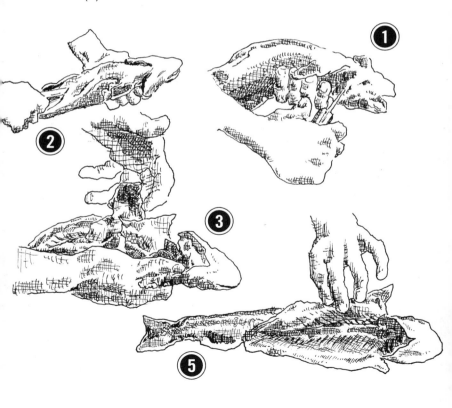

Barbecue what's left

(**1**) Stuff trout with tomatoes, onion, butter, lemon, lemon pepper. (**2**) Wrap in aluminum foil and toss onto the barbecue for about 10 minutes, turning after five minutes. (**3**) Accept compliments of grateful neighbors.

How to steak and fillet a 30-pound salmon

(**1**) Cut five 2-inch steaks first. Starting behind gill plate, cut through fish on one side from belly to backbone, using a large, sharp knife with serrated heel. (**2**) Saw through backbone with serrated edge. (**3**) Set steaks aside. (**4**) Now switch to an eight-inch fillet knife for the last 20 to 24 inches of fish. (**5**) Holding knife parallel to rib bones, make deep cut along backbone until you feel ribs. (**6**) Run knife along ribs in direction of tail, slicing meat away. (**7**) Once past ribs, run knife flat along backbone. (**8**) Flip the fillet over (skin side down), and lay knife flat along skin (optional). (**9**) Starting at top of tail, slice meat away from skin. (**10**) Now you're ready for barbecue or broiling. For steaks, paint with canola oil, cover in lemon pepper, and throw on grill. Don't overcook–

5 minutes per inch of thickness is plenty. Meat will flake with fork when done. For fillets, cover with canola oil or melted butter, season with salt and pepper or lemon pepper and the juice from a lemon wedge, and broil for 5 minutes per inch.

CHAPTER 43

THE JOY OF COMPOST: HOW TO MAKE YOUR OWN COMPOST BIN

Nothing is better for amending the heavy, clay soils common to the Western states than nutrient-rich organic matter. It helps everything from worms to tomatoes grow big and plump. (We hope the worms won't be in your tomatoes.)

Materials:

4 posts, 4' x 4" x 4"

16 furring strips, 3' x 1" x 1"

24 treated cedar boards, 1" x 6" x 3'

24 spacer blocks, 1" x 2" x 1"

1 sheet ⅜-inch plywood, 3' x 3'

Instructions

(**1**) Build your compost bin about three feet cubed.
(**2**) Sink the four corner posts one foot deep. (**3**) Tack
furring strips onto the two inside-facing surfaces of
each 4" x 4", spaced 1⅛" apart. (**4**) On three sides,
slide in 1" x 6" boards between furring strips. Between
each board, place a spacer block on each end. Repeat
until you reach the top of the post. (**5**) The plywood
sheet will act as your compost bin "door," giving you
easy access when you want to turn the pile or shovel
out finished compost.

What to dump into your compost bin

OLD POTTING SOIL

PULLED WEEDS

(**1**) If it's organic and belongs to the veg-
etable kingdom, it's got compost potential. (**2**) However, never put meat, cooking oil, grease, eggshells, or dairy products in the compost pile. They lead to
really bad smells, and really bad visitors
(rat-tailed types or furry, masked bandits).
(**3**) Dump in old potting soil, weeds
you've pulled (unless they have ripe
seeds), twigs, plant stalks. (**4**) Empty

your coffee grounds and paper filters right into your compost pile. (**5**) Be sure to dump in your leaves and grass clippings (but don't dump any clippings that have been treated with weed killer). (**6**) You can add up to 10% shredded newspapers. (**7**) Add about a cup of 10-6-4 fertilizer every two feet, every two months. It will speed things up nicely. (**8**) Composting requires oxygen and water. If the weather gets dry, give the pile a shot from the hose. (**9**) Turn your compost weekly with a pitchfork or shovel. A heinous rotten-egg or hideous ammonia odor means you haven't been doing your job. Toss in some veggie scraps to decrease alkalinity. (**10**) Your compost is ready when it's dark brown and crumbly and smells rich and earthy. Just open the door and scoop out the black gold. (**11**) Similar compost sells for about $5 a yard at the garden store. Got any entrepreneurial spirit?

COFFEE GROUNDS

GRASS CLIPPINGS

YOUR COMPOST

CHAPTER 44
HOW TO HELP KEEP THE NORTHWEST CLEAN AND GREEN

Steps for clean rivers

1. Stencil curb drains near your house with reminder: "Dump No Waste. Drains to Stream."

2. Avoid overfilling your gas tank.
3. Recycle used oil and oil filters. (Oil spilled from one small engine can produce an eight-acre oil slick.)
4. Use oil-absorbent materials, not detergents, to clean up spills.
5. Don't overfertilize your lawn. Use lawn chemicals sparingly, if at all.
6. Conserve water.
7. Buy food produced using sustainable farming. Produce marked with Food Alliance stickers is grown in the Northwest using minimal pesticides and good soil/water techniques.

Garden organically and manually

1. Fertilize with manure (after a little composting you may learn to love the smell).
2. Use plenty of composted yard debris for plantings.
3. For weeds, replace the concept "spray" with the concept "pull."
4. Relearn the art of raking leaves.
5. Push that hand mower. It's easier on your ears. Not to mention the air you breathe.

Invite a lady over

Start each spring by releasing a thousand ladybugs in your yard. Most nurseries stock beneficial bugs (ironically, sometimes they're right next to the chemicals). Not only do ladybugs eat every aphid in sight, but they feel a lot better on your skin than pesticides do.

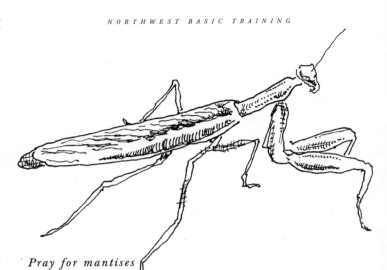

Pray for mantises

Bring on the ultimate predator. The praying mantis is a three-inch eating machine. Just set out a praying mantis egg pod in the crotch of a tree. Basically, the mantises will do the rest.

CHAPTER 45
DEAL WITH DISASTER

Learn to live with rattlers: Rattlesnake short course

The western rattlesnake, recognizable by its triangular viper head, is the Northwest's only poisonous snake. It's found in desert areas, often under rocky shelves.

How to behave in rattlesnake country

1. Don't poke your hand into dark places.

2. You'll never forget the sound of a rattling tail. This is your warning to "give me some space, or else." And this aggressive snake means what it says.

3. If you do hear a rattle, freeze. Back slowly away. If you haven't been bitten, jump for joy. Or,

---

Snakebite treatment

1. As with all bites, clean the wound.

2. Use a venom-sucking device from your first aid kit only if you are in backcountry, and medical help is not forthcoming. (Hint: Don't use your mouth. The old "slash, suck, and spit" technique is pure Hollywood fiction, not safe for you or the victim.)

3. Keep bitten limb immobilized, and below heart level. Keep victim calm.

4. Get the heck to a doctor.

Learn to live with rattlers: Earthquake short course

Experts say the Northwest is way overdue for "the big one." A monster, Richter-scale thumping 7.5+ quake could shake the Northwest at any time. The great Oregon quake of 1700 would have measured

8+. And in 2001 a 6.8 quake hit Olympia and Seattle, rattling residents as far away as Salem, Oregon.

Earthquake survival kit

I GALLON DRINKING WATER
PER PERSON IN HOUSEHOLD

LEATHERMAN MULTIPURPOSE TOOL

COLLAPSIBLE SHOVEL

FIRST AID KIT

FLASHLIGHT

PORTABLE RADIO

FRESH BATTERIES

CANNED FOOD

BLANKETS

CANDLES, MATCHES

1. Use common sense and, with luck, you'll emerge from the quake with nothing worse than a few loose fillings.
2. If you think you're in a quake, you are.
3. Duck, cover, hold on. Get under desk or table.
4. Stay away from glass.
5. Stay away from brick fireplaces.
6. Hope you're not in an elevator. That's freaky.

Pre-quake prep

1. Strap your water heater to studs in wall with metal strapping and lag screws.
2. Secure tall furniture to wall with metal L brackets.
3. Install latch devices on cabinet doors to secure dishes and glassware.

What to do during an oil spill

A major oil spill could happen, be it a diesel truck overturning on a cliff above a stream or an oil tanker run aground. The following are basic tactics to employ:

1. Collarlike booms contain oil and keep it from spreading.
2. Smaller skimmers, resembling giant vacuums, suck oil from the water.
3. Chemicals break up oil.
4. Various absorbent devices soak up oil.
5. Oil may be burned off.
6. Polyethylene recovery belts soak up the spill and are wrung out.
7. Spun-glass collectors, treated with oil-loving surfactants, may be deployed.
8. Resin-impregnated, recycled paper soaks up yet more oil and is then burned.
9. Beach cleaning continues for two to three years.
10. Birds are usually vicitims of spills. They are cleaned with mild detergents, water, and plenty of patience.

NOTE: Just one gallon of oil in one million gallons of water would kill half of all baby Dungeness crabs present.

What to do if you meet a cougar

1. Fine-tune your senses in cougar country. Cougars are stealthy and quiet, although they may snarl.

2. Don't run. That's true when other predatory animals attack as well. There are two reasons: Running triggers the chase instinct, and you'll never outrun a cougar (even an old, fat, three-legged one).

3. Act bigger than life. Spread your arms. Wave your arms. Wave your coat.

4. Yell. Talk nasty. Speak forcefully. It may confuse and discourage a cougar. But don't scream in a high pitched voice—the cougar may mistake you for a frightened deer.

5. If you have children with you, pick them up. They are probably the target, plus picking them up makes you both appear larger.

6. Back away slowly. Be glad you're not the one carrying the steaks for the campground barbecue.

What to do if you find a cougar on your back

1. Once attacked by a cougar, you only have one choice. Fight like hell. Playing dead only works with grizzlies, and they don't live in the Northwest.

2. Nail the cougar in the face with pepper spray. (Pepper spray also discourages bears, making it a backcountry idea that's sound.)

3. Use any club you have handy. A heavy flashlight works well. A stout limb can also beat off a cougar. Or grab a large rock.

4. If nothing else is at hand, fight with your feet and your fists. Try to strike the animal's nose. Protect your flabby underbelly.

5. Seek medical treatment, even if you don't think your wounds are serious. Any animal attack requires antibiotics and rabies evaluation.

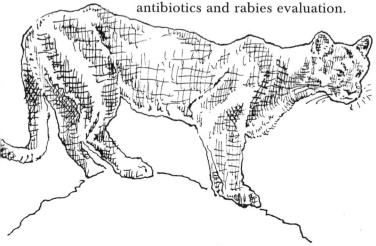

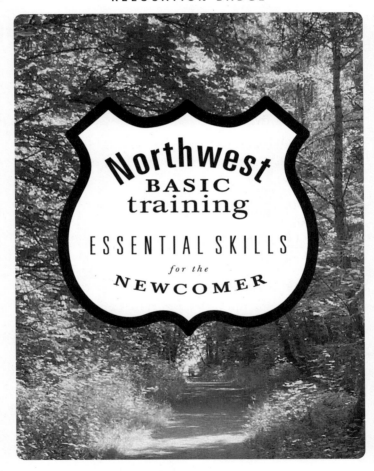

Northwest
BASIC
training
ESSENTIAL SKILLS
for the
NEWCOMER

*Awarded if you have accomplished at least
four of the following:*

- ❏ Do you own a piece of original glass art made by a Northwest artist?

- ❏ Do you have your own mug reserved at the local brewpub?

- ❏ Do at least five baristas know you by name?

- ❏ Do you always remember when to set out your recycling bins?

- ❏ Can you recite at least one stanza from "Louie, Louie"? (Mumbling doesn't count.)

- ❏ Do you have at least two favorite spots for watching whale migrations?

- ❏ Do you know where to drive your vehicle onto a ferry?

- ❏ Have you split a cord of wood?

- ❏ Do you consider eagles almost a family pet?

- ❏ Can you hit the fog lights on your car without looking?

log house

wine / garlic and
Basil / Pesto

Mud Puddle

STORY

SECTION	NATIVE
No. 3	**NORTHWESTERNER**

And you thought you knew everything about the Northwest. But even salty-dog residents of 60 years, born with Chinook blood in their veins, who brew their own beer and sail the San Juans, can stand to learn a few things. Or maybe you just want to be able to sit back, nod when outsiders tell you how jealous they are of Northwest residents, and bask in the glory of having rain-forest roots. Glean a few tidbits from this section, and use them as you may.

WAYS TO PASS ON NORTHWEST KNOWLEDGE:

❏ Tell Sasquatch-sighting yarn for 400th time.

❏ Take visiting relatives to bald eagle nesting site.

❏ Organize film festival, kicked off with showing of comedy classic, *Animal House*."

❏ Lead a drift boat down a river. without hitting a rock.

WAYS TO SHOW OFF NORTHWEST KNOWLEDGE:

❏ Fillet a salmon in under a minute, leaving less than 1/16" of meat on bones.

❏ Remove snowshoes from wall and point out notches from "avalanche in '77."

❏ Recall starting five of Blazers and Sonics championship basketball teams.

❏ Recite cowboy poem you wrote, while on horseback.

WAYS TO ACQUIRE MORE NORTHWEST KNOWLEDGE:

❏ Read this book.

❏ Attend ceremonial totem-pole carving.

❏ Spend a week on a mountain with a Mazama guide.

❏ Buy your own microbrewery.

CHAPTER 46
WHAT TO DO WITH
A BEACHED WHALE

---

1. Assume the beached whale is an orca, not a 300-pound sunburned tourist.

2. First of all, observe the tide. The whale probably got stranded in the shallows on an outgoing tide while chasing a seal or large fish. Whales sometimes also beach themselves if disoriented by parasites or disease.

3. If possible, recruit the authorities for help.

4. Then start trenching around the great beast. Trenching will allow water to seep up to the whale.

5. It's vital to keep the whale wet. Have someone continuously pour buckets of seawater over the whale as you orchestrate the tow.

6. Ropes can damage the whale's skin, so secure your tow rope over its tail, first carefully wrapping the rope in towels or a blanket.

7. An all-terrain vehicle or even a passing horse can help with the tow task. A small whale may weigh 10,000 pounds.

8. Don't get anywhere near the massive jaws. Killer whales normally aren't harmful to people, but an injured animal may lash out.

9. Ideally, let the tide do the bulk of the pushing. Once the tide starts coming in, let it float the big critter.

10. Heave, ho, give it a tow. Gently tow backwards with the rope. ATV, horse, and people are going to have to get wet. Very wet. Release whale in the surf.

Desperate circumstances: beached gray whale

SCENARIO | Occasionally a dead gray whale will show up on one of our beaches. These are three courses of action:

PLAN A
Leave the stinking carcass to be disposed of by sand fleas, crabs, and seagulls. This should take only, oh, eight or nine years.

PLAN B
Bury the behemoth. Dig a big ditch. Push the unfortunate creature in with a bulldozer. And then watch the tide uncover it in a day or two.

PLAN C
Carefully set explosives to blast all 30 tons of blubber into oblivion. And all over every car, truck, boat, and beachcomber within a quarter of a mile. If such an activity is ever in progress when you're near the beach, head for the sand hills.

CHAPTER 47
TRACK AND SHOOT AN ELK

Track elk

(**1**) Select hunting area in Roosevelt elk range, near river bottom. (**2**) Watch for broken branches. (**3**) Observe any aspens with blackened, stripped trunks, a sign of feeding elk. (**4**) Look for trees rubbed bare by elk working velvet off horns. (**5**) Notice hoof prints. They are larger than deer's but similar in appearance. (**6**) Observe elk scat. If it's moist, elk were recently in the vicinity. (**7**) Remain still. Otherwise, the elk's keen senses will detect you.

How to compose a classic shot

(**1**) Wait for the right light. Ideally, sunrise, because it's not only interesting light, but the best time to see elk. (**2**) Crawl on your belly over rocks, into brambles, through scat. That last part is good reason to keep your mouth closed during the stalk. (**3**) Focus on clearing in path of bull elk. (**4**) Don't shoot until elk is in the clear. (**5**) Aim at elk's shoulder, make sure elk fills your viewfinder. (**6**) Trip shutter.

Gear list

❏ NIKON N60 OR SIMILAR SLR CAMERA

❏ 200MM OR 300MM LENS

❏ POLARIZING FILTER

❏ 400 SPEED FILM

❏ CAMOUFLAGE CLOTHING (THOUGH NOT A GOOD IDEA DURING HUNTING SEASON)

❏ COW ELK URINE SCENT. (SPLASH THIS LIBERALLY ALL OVER YOUR BODY LIKE COLOGNE. YOU'LL BLEND RIGHT IN, AT LEAST UNTIL YOU GET TO THE BREWPUB.)

CHAPTER 48
HOW TO BECOME BIGFOOT: MAKE SNOWSHOES

Shoemaking

1. Craft the bindings.
   - Carve out a piece of leather.
   - Toe flap and two side flaps should fold up.
   - Cut lacing holes.
   - Two holes in bottom for rawhide or nylon straps, which criss-cross heel and tie in front of boot.

2. Carve snowshoe frame.
   ○ Cut a length of tree about 30" long.
   ○ Strip bark with drawknife.
   ○ Hand-hew two straight poles. Plane wood until
     about ¾" or 1" in diameter.
3. Soak wood. Steam wood to impregnate with moisture before trying to bend. Otherwise, it's "snap,
   crackle, pop" and no more snowshoes.
4. Bend poles. Insert in jig
   frame and hold in place
   with C-clamps.
5. Dry for a couple of
   weeks.
6. Insert crossbars.
7. Cut rawhide strips.
8. Lace snowshoes as
   shown.
9. Varnish wood portions.

Tools and materials:

WOOD STOCK:
QUAKING ASPEN OR SPRUCE

AX, VERY SHARP

DRAWKNIFE (TO REMOVE BARK)

PLANE

HALF DOZEN C-CLAMPS

JIGS (DEVICES TO BEND WOOD)

RAWHIDE

STEAMER OR SOAKER

LACER'S HOOK

SHELLAC

How to make rawhide:

(**1**) Skin cow, elk, or moose. (**2**) Stretch skin on frame. Scrape off all hide. (**3**) Let dry. Do not wet, as this weakens rawhide. (**4**) Cut in strips to use for snow-

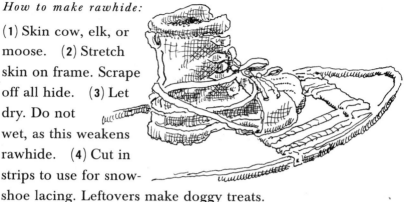

shoe lacing. Leftovers make doggy treats.

DECOR TIP | These traditional Northwest snowshoes double as decor—just cross them over your mantel after a long day of snowshoeing.

*How to build a snow cave
(in case your snowshoes fall apart):*

(**1**) If you are caught in a winter storm, look for a steep snowdrift, with firm snow. Powder won't do. (**2**) Use one of your showshoes to dig an entryway into the snow. (**3**) Dig in about three or four feet. (**4**) Then dig upward, and create a large, flat space for sitting/sleeping. (**5**) Fashion a concave roof. (**6**) Lay your ever-handy space blanket on snow to retain body heat and stay dry.   **(7)** Poke vent hole from ceiling to outside air using back of snowshoe. Leave snowshoe in vent hole, wiggling occasionally to keep it open.

CHAPTER 49
**HOW TO BUCK A SAW
AND MAKE A BUCK**

Buck a saw

(**1**) Make sure tree is horizontal.
(**2**) The crosscut saw cuts on
both motions, the push and the
pull.   (**3**) Lube the saw with
light oil. Keep it wet to help thin
the tree sap and minimize binding.
(**4**) Develop a rhythm and keep it going.
(**5**) Cut several 18-inch lengths. This is the ideal size
to split for firewood.   (**6**) Repeat steps 1 through 5
several hundred times. Strip naked and admire mus-
cular body in mirror.

Now make a buck

(**1**) Split the lengths of wood.   (**2**) Season the pieces
for six months in dry area, away from your house
(piling firewood near house encourages termites and
other wood-destroying insects).   (**3**) Sell as prime firewood. Charge $140/cord.

Logger lingo

WIDOWMAKER—Loose tree limb, needing only wind to become lethal projectile. **JILLPOKED**—Not sexual slang, but rather term for log with one end buried, one end up in the air. **GYPPO**—Old world term for independent logging contractor. New world term for deal you struck for new chainsaw. **PEAVEY**—Type of logging tool: a pry bar with hook attached. **SNAG**—Standing dead tree. Also called "home" by bald eagles and woodpeckers. **CALKS**—Those fashionable, spike-soled boots loggers wear. **SNOOSE**—Chewin' tobacco.

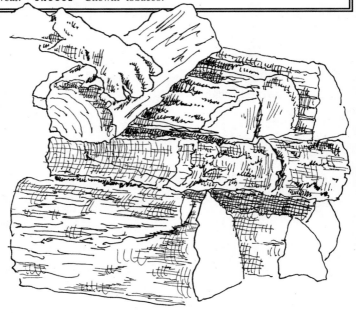

CHAPTER 50
**CRAFT YOUR OWN
DUGOUT CANOE**

Raw materials:

Giant trunk of red cedar (you may have to travel back in time to find a perfect 12- or 14-foot section of red cedar log lying around).

Method:

(**1**) Peel bark. (**2**) Make a long Y cut at the stern and the bow to help guide your cuts and establish craft's shape. (**3**) Shape the keel using adze and ax. (**4**) Roll log over. (Unless you

Tools:

VARIOUS CHISELS

ADZE (ANCIENT WOOD-CHIPPING TOOL)

DYNAMITE (JUST KIDDING)

POWER SAW
(IF YOU DON'T WANT TO CHEAT, USE AN AX)

DRAWKNIFE FOR BARK STRIPPING

WISHFUL THINKING

RIVER ROCKS

recently won the Ms. or Mr. Olympia contest, you may need a hoist for this.) (**5**) Make cuts about two inches in from sides, all the way to the Y cut. (**6**) Remove heartwood. Chip it out. Whack it out. Burn it out. This will take awhile...like, a month. Controlled burning was used by ancient tribes. You'll have to experiment to see how easy "controlling" it

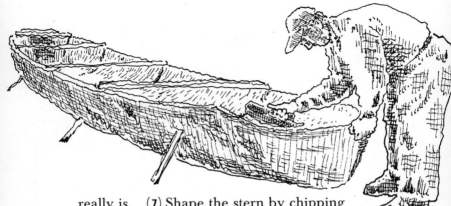

really is. (**7**) Shape the stern by chipping
away, hour after hour. Take a break and rent
the video *Last of the Mohicans* to renew your spirit.
(**8**) Fill with water. (**9**) Add hot rocks. (**10**) As
steam softens sides, add wider and wider stretching
posts to create the stabilizing bulge in the middle.
(**11**) Decorate outside of finished canoe. We suggest
red and black Native American designs.

    If you actually finish a canoe, it may take over a
year. Oops, that may cost you your job. But you will
have given the Northwest a true treasure. We thank
you in advance for your sacrifice.

CHAPTER 51
WINCH YOURSELF
BACK UP THE MOUNTAIN

SCENARIO | You're off-road. You're in charge of your own destiny. You can go anywhere, do anything. You're...stuck. Trapped in that lovely goo commonly known as deep shit. Assuming you can summon help, you'll need to:

(**1**) Use a tow strap or chain. Always make sure a tow strap is one that's made for that purpose, with minimal stretch to it. Otherwise, if it breaks, it could become a whip on steroids. (**2**) Understand where to hook it up. Secure the chain to your frame (not the bumper, unless you want it yanked off faster than a bad tooth strung to a door). (**3**) Secure the other end to the rescue vehicle. (**4**) As the rescue vehicle slowly backs up, press your gas pedal gently. Spinning your wheels will only dig you in deeper.
(**5**) Remove chains.

Winch yourself out of trouble

If you can't contact help, you can either (A) wait anywhere from two hours to two years for someone to happen by, or (B) use that Warn self-recovery electric winch you were smart enough to buy when you got your vehicle.

1. Put the winch on free spool.
2. Connect the remote control.
3. Put on your leather gloves.
4. Find a stout tree in the direction you'd like to winch.
5. Wrap the tree protector around trunk.
6. Attach a snatch block.
7. Attach a shackle with D-ring to the snatch block. Tighten by hand, then back off a quarter-turn.
8. Return to the winch. Grasp the hook and begin pulling out winch cable (it's a wire rope, part of the reason you need gloves).
9. Pull the cable slowly until it can reach the tree.
10. Insert winch hook into D-ring.

SAFETY CHECK: Never straddle the winch rope. During winching, make sure everyone in your party is at least 6 feet away to either side. You may drape a coat over winch cable...to absorb shock in rare event it breaks.

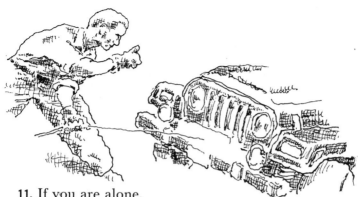

11. If you are alone,
    you can bring the remote into your vehicle.

12. Start the winching process by pushing the lever.

13. Once your vehicle secures a purchase, put it in
    park and set the parking brake.

14. Back off the remote to form slack in the winch
    cable.

15. Remembering not to straddle the cable, disengage
    the winch hook from the D-ring.

16. Use the remote to roll the cable back onto the
    winch drum.

17. Assist the direction with one gloved hand.

18. When hook is about 5 feet from the fairlead, lay
    the cable on the ground.

19. Inch cable onto drum.

    CAUTION: It's best to attach a strap to hook as you respool the cable, and then hold the
    strap rather than the hook. Fairlead where cable goes into winch is dangerous...keep
    fingers away!

CHAPTER 52
HOW TO SQUEEZE WATER FROM A ROCK

During one of your forays to the high desert, you've wandered off and found yourelf getting parched.

Here's what to do:

LOOK FOR A POSSIBLE WATER SOURCE

Stream

Spring

Groundwater

Rain

Snow

Ice

Dew

Succulent plants, such as cacti

Fruits

Catch basins (porous lava rock areas)

Water trapped at the base of cliffs

CAUTION: Remember, any water you find in the wilderness must be purified. Carry any one of the multitude of purifiers available at outdoor stores.

Make a solar still

Turn a plastic sheet into a water machine using:

5' x 5' plastic sheet (cut open a large plastic bag if it's all you have) — Bucket or any other watertight vessel — 4-foot length of tubing — Rocks — Small shovel

1. Dig a pit about 4 feet across and 3 feet deep.

2. Place the bucket in the bottom of the pit.

3. Place one end of tube in bucket and extend other end up to ground level.

4. Lay plastic sheeting across hole.

5. Place rocks or dirt all around outside of sheet.

6. Place a single fist-sized rock in middle of plastic.

As the sun gets hot, the evaporating water in the air is trapped on the underside of the plastic and runs into the bucket.

CHAPTER 53
**TEACH AN OLD SLUG
NEW TRICKS**

Slugs make inexpensive pets. Try these tricks:

ROLL OVER—Slide a sheet of paper under your slug, and flip it into the air. **SPEAK**—Unfortunately, your slug's language skills are limited. **WRITE YOUR NAME**—As your slug crawls down the sidewalk at night, gently nudge it with a pencil until it spells out every letter in your name with slime. Now flash a light on the slime trail. Squeal with joy as you admire your pet's handiwork. **FETCH**—See "Speak." **DINNER**—Place your slug on your least favorite relative's most prized plant and watch it munch.

EMERGENCY NOTE: Should your slug escape and lead an army of its cousins to your garden, be prepared.

Slug defenses

(**1**) Outline your tender garden veggies and strawberries with slug bait. Be sure to check the label to make sure it's safe for other pets.   (**2**) Sink a couple bowls of beer (certainly not a Northwest microbrew—try Hamms) level with the ground. Slugs are suckers for a night of drinking, after which they're too drunk to escape the bowl.

Sluggo ID Guide

BANANA SLUG.
ARIOLIMAX COLUMBIANUS. 6–10".
LIGHT TO DARK BROWN, OFTEN MOTTLED WITH BLACK SPOTS. SLITHERS ON MOIST FOREST FLOORS.

LEOPARD, OR GREAT GRAY GARDEN SLUG. LIMAX MAXIMUS. 4".
GRAY/BROWN WITH BLACK SPOTS/STRIPES. THIS IS THE SLUG THAT EATS PRETTY MUCH EVERYTHING IN YOUR GARDEN.

EUROPEAN SLUG.
ARION ATER. 2–5".
REDDISH-BROWN TO BLACK. HAS A VORACIOUS APPETITE FOR STRAWBERRIES. FOUND IN STRAWBERRY FIELDS, GARDENS.

BLUE TOP SNAIL.
CALLIOSTOMA LIGATUM. 1".
BROWN, WITH CONICAL, WHORLED SHELL. A SLUG WITH A HOUSE, FOUND UNDER ROCKS AT LOW TIDE.

CHAPTER 54
HOW TO CATCH TROUT ON A FLY YOU TIE

Basic trout fly-fishing gear list

8-FOOT, 5-WEIGHT FLY ROD

REEL

WICKER CREEL (DOUBLES AS FIREPLACE DECOR)

NEOPRENE WADERS (CINCH A BELT AROUND THE WAIST—HELPS YOU FLOAT IF YOU TRIP)

WADING BOOTS

NET (GET THE ULTRA-CLASSY WOOD-HANDLED VERSION)

CHEST PACK TO HOLD YOUR FLIES, BEEF JERKY, ETC.

GOOD-LOOKIN' HAT

FLY LINE

FLIES

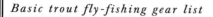

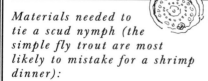

Materials needed to tie a scud nymph (the simple fly trout are most likely to mistake for a shrimp dinner):

VISE

SMALL SCISSORS

THREADS

HOOKS

CEMENT

BOBBIN (HOLDS SPOOL OF THREAD)

THIN COPPER WIRE

HOOK

DUBBING MATERIAL (FUZZY STUFF FOR THE BODY)

HACKLE (FEATHER)

ZIPLOC BAG

How to tie one on:

(1) Place a #14 hook in a fly-tier's vise (smaller is better with finicky trout). (2) Wrap black thread on back half of hook. Start at a 45-degree angle, then wrap thread back over itself. (3) Tie in some brown whisks from your hackle. (4) Tie in a strip of plastic 2 inches long by ⅛ inch wide, cut from a ziploc bag. (If you can believe it, this will imitate the shell-like covering freshwater shrimp have.) (5) Tie in piece of thin copper wire. (6) Tie in dubbing material. Wax your fingers and kind of work it into a puffy mess. (7) Wind the dubbing forward. This becomes the shrimp's body. (8) Tie off dubbing. (9) Pull the hackle forward. (10) Tie it off. Trim front and sides, leaving "feet" at bottom. (11) Pull plastic forward. (12) Wrap and tie off. Trim. (13) Wrap copper wire several times around hook, back to front, to "segment" body. (14) Add drop of cement to head. (15) Now go fool some fish. Just

cast nymph into a small stream. Let it drift
naturally behind a boulder. Set the
hook when you feel a tug.

*If you're a true native, "catch" means
"release"*

(**1**) Handle your trophy gently. Wet
your hands before touching fish.
(**2**) Don't squeeze the fish.   (**3**) Snap
photo.   (**4**) Gently work
hook out of fish's mouth.
Barbless hooks work best.
(**5**) Release fish. To revive your catch, gently move it
back and forth in the water. This will get its gills
working and help it recover.   (**6**) Wonder why you
just purchased $400 barbecue grill.

CHAPTER 55
**WANT TO REALLY KNOW
THE NORTHWEST? WALK IT.**

This crude map is all you need to walk from one
end of the Pacific Northwest to the other. Just stay on
the marked Pacific Coast Trail. Lewis and Clark, eat
your hearts out.

The Pacific Crest Trail map

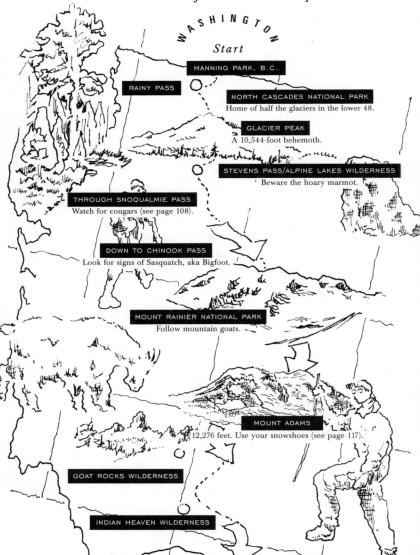

WASHINGTON

Start

MANNING PARK, B.C.

RAINY PASS

NORTH CASCADES NATIONAL PARK
Home of half the glaciers in the lower 48.

GLACIER PEAK
A 10,544-foot behemoth.

STEVENS PASS/ALPINE LAKES WILDERNESS
Beware the hoary marmot.

THROUGH SNOQUALMIE PASS
Watch for cougars (see page 108).

DOWN TO CHINOOK PASS
Look for signs of Sasquatch, aka Bigfoot.

MOUNT RAINIER NATIONAL PARK
Follow mountain goats.

MOUNT ADAMS
12,276 feet. Use your snowshoes (see page 117).

GOAT ROCKS WILDERNESS

INDIAN HEAVEN WILDERNESS

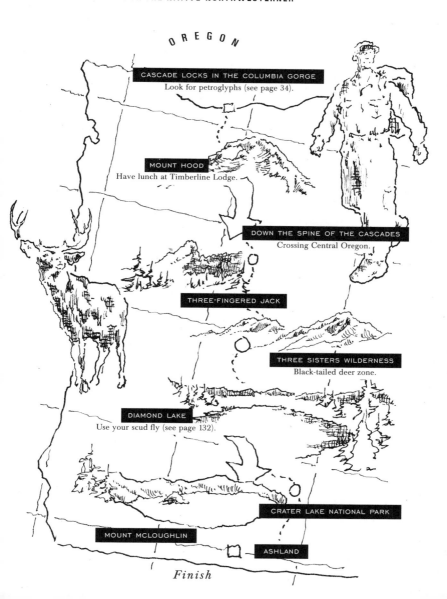

O R E G O N

CASCADE LOCKS IN THE COLUMBIA GORGE
Look for petroglyphs (see page 34).

MOUNT HOOD
Have lunch at Timberline Lodge.

DOWN THE SPINE OF THE CASCADES
Crossing Central Oregon.

THREE-FINGERED JACK

THREE SISTERS WILDERNESS
Black-tailed deer zone.

DIAMOND LAKE
Use your scud fly (see page 132).

CRATER LAKE NATIONAL PARK

MOUNT MCLOUGHLIN

ASHLAND

Finish

At this point, you are either dead or a new person. You are one with the Northwest wilderness. You are a native Northwesterner down to your blistered and battered toes. Congratulations.

Advanced Hiker's Tip

Carve your own walking stick. It will:

Help stabilize you on high trails;

Act as a probe when you're fording streams;

Push aside blackberry thorns and nettles;

Thwart rattlesnakes or spiders.

Start by choosing a stout wood such as hickory. Strip the bark. Drill a half-inch hole about five inches from the top. Attach a leather strap. Coat stick with varnish.

CHAPTER 56
WRITING
"THE" SCREENPLAY

Before you begin, consider the essentials of a great screenplay:

– CHARACTER –

Well-rounded, interesting characters are the heart of all the films you care about. Write based on people you know or have met. Develop your ear for dialogue—eavesdrop on the train or on the bus.

– CONFLICT –

How people come into conflict with
each other is the essence of all drama.

– PLOT –

You need an idea of how the action will progress in your film.
For example, your plot scenario might read:

A pair of beachcombers, strolling on a windswept beach in Olympic National Park, build a beach fire and discover a glass fishing float. Scribbled onto the glass, in blood, is a plea for help. It's from a woman who says she's being held captive somewhere in the park. Thus starts a desperate quest to find the woman. Just when they begin to think the float's message may have been a prank, a ranger receives a lock of the woman's hair and a ransom note: "You have 12 hours. Either I find $100,000 wrapped in black plastic in the outhouse, or you find her buried beneath a fir tree."

– SETTING –

The Northwest's lush forests, national parks, and quaint cities can provide the kind of happy backdrops where audiences love to lose themselves—see *Kindergarten Cop* or *Sleepless in Seattle*, for example. But all that rain and gloom can be conducive to creating your own kind of Northwest noir, too.

Let your screenplay take form

Learn to write with plot progression, dialogue, and the camera in mind. Typically the form contains three acts. Screenplays are about 120 pages long.

– ACT I –	– ACT II –	– ACT III –
30 pages	60 pages	30 pages
Set up.	Conflict.	Conclusion.
Basically, in the first act you define your characters, how they relate to each other, and what they'll be doing.	This is where things happen to your characters. Good things. Bad things. Man vs. man. Man vs. nature. Your characters vault their various hurdles here.	Also called resolution. This is where you wrap it up. Make sure you tie up all those loose ends. Is there an evil twist? A happy ending?

Using the plot scenario from page 137, here is how you might script your opening scene

---

EXT. WASHINGTON BEACH/CAMPFIRE –

NIGHT– CLOSE ON KURT

Greg and Kurt throwing clams into pot of water.

KURT
See that float?

TIGHT SHOT:

GREG
The green one? Grab it, would ya?

KURT'S POV:

KURT
It's covered with something...blood!

CHAPTER 57
**HOW TO BECOME A COWBOY POET
OR A FISHER POET**

What makes a good cowboy poet:

(1) Like a good country western song, a cowboy poem needs two things: good delivery, plenty of angst.

(2) Cowboy poem technique: lots of rhyming. Study the following:

> On the run, he's forced to hide,
> In yonder cave, he dove inside.
> And as the lawman's shadow fell,
> A strategy formed, clear as a bell.
> "I'll shoot my way out," he told himself,
> "But first I'll nap, on yonder shelf."

(**3**) You don't have to write well. Just write often. That's the key to improving your prose. (**4**) A little work on your rhyming here, a few syllables off your meter there, and you will get better. (**5**) Perform live. Trade in your spurs for pens. Then find the next open mike opportunity.

Keys for the fisher poet:

(**1**) Also surfacing in Northwestern cafes and brewpubs are fisher poets. These deepwater anglers have plenty of time on their hands between trips to sea. They pour the soul of their brief sojourns into writing about the Pacific. (**2**) If you've ever wet a line, you have what it takes to take up this rhyming hobby. (**3**) Sample fisher poem:

> I was suckin' fumes when the big "hali" hit.
> She turned me around, slowed me a bit.
> Burned off more line, my reel was a smokin'
> That was one big fish, and I ain't a jokin'.

(**4**) No one really knows what a fisher poet is. So, declare yourself one. Feel free to express yourself. Match verse with Alaska, Oregon, and Washington fisher poets every February in Astoria, Oregon.

CHAPTER 58
HOW TO RIDE YOUR BIKE TO WORK

Go from $120 a month for gas to $0. And do the same for parking.

Here's how:

(**1**) For a taste of the two-wheeled commute, start on "Ride your bike to work day." These special days are set up to encourage new cyclists, and parking is often provided.   (**2**) Check with your employer as to whether you can store your bike in the office or need to find special on-street parking.   (**3**) Observe designated bike parking areas.   (**4**) Carry heavy cable chain or U-lock. Locks/chains need to stand up to bolt cutters.

(**5**) Obey all traffic signals. While you may think you can see all the oncoming obstacles, motorcycles and low-profile sports cars are extremely hard to see in poor light conditions. A bicyclist may not survive an encounter with either. (**6**) Wear multiple reflectors: shoes, strips on rain parka, reflective patch on back of helmet. (**7**) Avoid going to work with a "brown stripe" up your back. Rainy days create slick, slurry mixtures that are picked up by your bike tires and slopped across your back as you ride. The resulting brown stripe is unfashionable, even on casual Fridays. Use fenders and wear a raincoat. (**8**) Watch for parked cars. Car doors will be flung open when you have the least amount of room for error. (**9**) Remember you're not in Manhattan. Cyclists do not have the right of way over pedestrians. In fact, running over pedestrians is frowned upon in all circumstances.

CHAPTER 59
THE FINER POINTS OF CREATING YARD ART

How to be a chain-saw artiste:

1. Wear red suspenders.

2. Grow beard.

3. Pick out a hunk of wood. You want to find a dead cedar log, something you can scavenge without cutting down trees.

4. Now size it up. Let the wood speak to you.

5. Look for shapes or forms that might suggest the grizzled face of a salty dog or the beak of a pelican. Do you see a bear? An eagle? Of course you do.

6. Time to let 'er rip. Carve a very rough outline with a chain saw.

7. Make finesse cuts with chain saw. Be careful. Avoid knots. Remember, chain saws can bind or

buck. Don't put your face in the path of a chain-saw kickback!

8. Do your fine-tuning, if you can call it that, using a dimmel, a common wood-carving tool.

9. Paint features or leave raw.
10. Apply a mess of lacquer.
11. Plop finished work of art in your front yard and wait for neighbors to make you an offer—or call the cops.

How to turn trash metal into a weathervane in 60 minutes flat:

TOOLS AND MATERIALS:

RECYCLED JUNK METAL

CUTTING TORCH

WELDING TORCH

BALL-BEARING MOUNTING KNUCKLES (JUST TELL THE HARDWARE GUY YOU NEED SOMETHING TO MOUNT YOUR SCULPTURE ON SO IT WILL ROTATE FREELY WITH THE WIND)

METAL SUPPORT ROD
(HALF-INCH DIAMETER,
4 FEET LONG)

MOUNTING BRACKET

PATIENCE

The process:

1. Draw a design on a piece of recycled junk metal or copper. Copper is the coolest material to use because of the greenish patina it acquires.
2. Cut out your design. Roughly 18 inches in diameter is ideal—big enough to catch the wind, small enough to be tasteful (if that's possible).
3. Weld the rod to the bottom of your sculpture.
4. Run the other end of the rod through the pivot knuckle.
5. Insert the end of the rod into the mounting bracket.
6. Affix to fence, gutter, or roofline.
7. Now stand back and bask in the glory of the compliments your neighbors will heap upon your swollen head.

Design templates

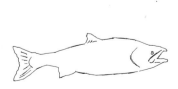
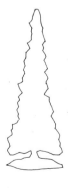

CHAPTER 60
MAKE A NORTHWEST ANTI-FASHION STATEMENT

HEADBAND OF WOVEN STRAW
INTERLACED WITH COLORED YARN

NATURAL SHELL EARRINGS
(FORMERLY INHABITED
BY SMALL INVERTEBRATES)

HEMP NECKLACE

FLEECE SWEATER,
MADE FROM 90%
RECYCLED GREEN-
PLASTIC POP BOTTLES

ALL-COTTON PANTS,
YARN-DYED (AN EARTH-
FRIENDLY PROCESS)

HIKING SOCKS,
ALL-NATURAL BLEND
OF COTTON AND
ALPACA FIBERS

SHOES MADE
FROM RECYCLED
TIRES AND CANVAS

"Earth-Friendly"

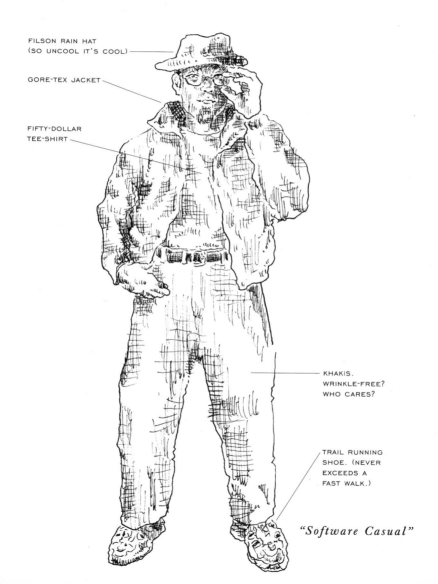

FILSON RAIN HAT
(SO UNCOOL IT'S COOL)

GORE-TEX JACKET

FIFTY-DOLLAR
TEE-SHIRT

KHAKIS.
WRINKLE-FREE?
WHO CARES?

TRAIL RUNNING
SHOE. (NEVER
EXCEEDS A
FAST WALK.)

"Software Casual"

CHAPTER 61
HOW TO BE AN AMATEUR BARISTA

(**1**) Turn your kitchen into a coffee shop. Send the kids out to play—it's coffee time.   (**2**) Have friends and neighbors line up in orderly fashion. No pushing. (**3**) Let them shout out orders. Your mind is now a steel trap.   (**4**) Field orders like an old pro. Never, under any circumstances, write a request down. This implies weakness at the espresso machine and will make guests nervous.   (**5**) When you make a "skinny" latte for your sister instead of a "breve," just accidentally on purpose forget to tell her. She could stand to lose a few pounds, anyway.   (**6**) Double cup all the drinks you make. You may burn the coffee, but you won't burn your customers.   (**7**)Always act confidently. When you make an error, simply say "that's a new bean I'm trying," or "funny, my last customer liked 16 shots of vanilla syrup."   (**8**) Don't be afraid to boast—"I insist on only the finest Ethiopian coffee... hand selected by the prime minister's personal barista."   (**9**) When you hear the words "vanilla latte, please" your fingers fly into action, taking these steps to perfection:

Brew the perfect vanilla latte

Grind coffee to an extra-fine consistency —
Measure out an 8-gram single shot. A double
would be—well, you do the math — Place in
strainer, tamp lightly — Make shot of espresso—turn brew machine so it will run hot
water through your coffee, and into glass
carafe — Fill a small steel pitcher about one-
third to one-half full of cold, fresh milk — Put
espresso machine on steaming mode — Open
steam valve briefly to clear condensed water
from line — Stick steam jet in your milk
pitcher — Heat to 160°F. Measure with fancy
thermometer you got
for Xmas — Create
frothy foam by putting
end of steam pipe near
milk's surface — Shut off
steam valve before
removing milk pitcher —
Pour an ounce of vanilla
syrup into your coffee cup — Pour espresso
into custom-glazed ceramic cup — Pour in
steamed milk — Spoon off some foam to
top it all off — Sprinkle on small layer of
finely ground milk-chocolate chips — Hand
cup to neighbor/customer — If they smile
and beg for more, quit your job and buy a
latte cart. Put it outside a busy grocery
store, and you're in business as a barista —
If they spit it out, keep your day job and
figure you'll be spending your money at
the coffeehouse.

TIP | Buy your coffee as whole
beans, and grind it at home. This
keeps it fresher and more flavorful.

Tools:

COFFEE GRINDER

ESPRESSO MACHINE

KNOWLEDGE OF COFFEE

VACUUM-PACKED BAGS OF
COFFEE BEANS

PLENTY OF SHINY STEEL
CUPS AND MEASURING
TOOLS

COFFEE THERMOMETER

TIP JAR ON YOUR KITCHEN
COUNTER

READY SMILE

FLAWLESS MEMORY (OR THE
ABILITY TO FAKE ONE)

CHAPTER 62
HOW TO CLIMB A NORTHWEST VOLCANO

(**1**) Identify the Cascade volcanic peak you'd like to climb and plan your route of attack. Get your map and guidebook at the local outdoor store. (**2**) Educate yourself about climbing. Consult local climbing clubs like The Mountaineers or the Mazamas. *Mountaineering: the Freedom of the Hills*, published by The Mountaineers, is the best text available. (**3**) Get in shape. Triathlon kind of shape. Run steps, use the stair-stepper at the club. Do it hour after hour after hour. Remember, too much is never enough. (**4**) Get the right gear.

(**5**) Pack a monster lunch the night before. Quick-grab foods are best. Stuff your pockets with the high-energy items (hard candy, energy bars, etc.). A high-carb meal the night before is essential. (**6**) Check the weather, and keep an eye on the sky. If you overhear seasoned climbers saying, "Only a moron would go up today," take that as a clue. Don't be afraid to call off a climb if weather may get unfavorable.

(**7**) Leave early. Northwest mountains are best climbed between late May and late August. In other words, during sunny weather. But sun softens snow.

A midnight start is not too early.   (**8**) Wear layers. You'll start to sweat quickly.   (**9**) Pace yourself. Constantly looking up from your slow, painful slog uphill only seems to push the summit farther and farther away. (**10**) When you summit, congratulate your partners. Grab those energy bars and attempt to eat. (High elevation and exhaustion may prohibit enjoyment of food.) Drink fluids. (**11**) Take those hero snapshots. You are on top of the world!   (**12**) Make careful descent of the most difficult upper portion of the mountain.   (**13**) Since going down is actually harder than going up, time for a controlled glissade. In other words, sit on a plastic bag. Take a deep breath. And GO! (But before you go, make sure your guide approves...you don't want to slide off a cliff and do a header into a grove of fir trees.)

NORTHWEST TRIVIA NOTE |
Did you know Oregon's Mount Hood is the most frequently climbed mountain in the world?

Basic climbing equipment list:

TWO PAIRS OF WOOL
BLEND SOCKS

BOOTS

GAITERS FOR THE BOOTS

WOOL OR NYLON PANTS

SYNTHETIC LONG UNDERWEAR, TOPS
AND BOTTOMS

FLEECE SWEATER (VEST OPTIONAL)

INSULATED PARKA (MUST BE ABLE TO
PULL ON OVER YOUR SWEATER)

WOOL GLOVES OR MITTS
(AVOID LEATHER SKI GLOVES—THEY'RE
WORTHLESS WHEN WET)

WOOL CAP

BALL CAP FOR SUN PROTECTION

SUNGLASSES

SUNSCREEN

WATERPROOF, BREATHABLE RAIN SUIT

HEADLAMP WITH EXTRA BATTERY

ICE AX

PLASTIC BAG

LOCATION RESCUE DEVICE (AT THE
RISK OF JINXING YOU,
THIS IS IN CASE OF AVALANCHE)

FOR THE MORE TECHNICAL EQUIPMENT,
REFER TO YOUR CLIMBING MANUAL.

What to do if volcano starts to rumble, with you on it

(1) If you're on the summit when the volcano blows, just give it up. You're toast. Literally.   (2) If the volcano hasn't blown, but you hear rumblings or feel vibrations, see steam, or smell sulfur...pay attention, they could be volcanic precursors. Take them seriously. Start your descent.   (3) Cover your mouth with a wet cloth to help filter out volcanic dust and ash. (4) Try and protect your head from flying rock as you descend.   (5) A full tilt glissade is in order if the mountain is blowing. Get on your butt and slide. (6) If you're off the mountain and in the path of lava, either get to higher ground on a neighboring slope, or put a body of water between you and the flow.

> CHAPTER 63
> **HELP FOR DREADED**
> **NORTHWEST AILMENTS**

Cabin fever

1. **GO EAST.** Once you get east of the Cascades, the number of sunny days per year nearly doubles.

2. **BATHE IN LIGHT.** High-intensity lamps have been known to help cure the blues.

3. **SEEK HARMONIOUS MUSIC.** Music soothes the soul, even in a downpour.

4. **STAY BUSY.** Rather than dwelling on the gray day, work on a jigsaw puzzle. Play chess. Watch a movie. Read a classic Northwest novel.

Snowboarder's wrist

1. Check for break. In the case of a wrist, it's hard to determine without an x-ray whether anything is broken. Can you say "hospital emergency room"? No break? Go to #2.

2. Ice for 20 minutes.

3. Take an anti-inflammatory, such as ibuprofen.

4. Wrap with Ace bandage.

Sailboarder's elbow

Also known as "Gorge tendonitis" because of the Columbia River Gorge's reputation as a sailboard mecca. it's caused by the wind grabbing your sailboard and tugging at your arms and elbows, thousands of times.

1. Ice the sore joint.
2. Take anti-inflammatory medication for a week.
3. Keep afflicted arm in sling for two weeks.

Surfer's shark bite

The great white attacks what it thinks is a seal—like a surfer in a black wetsuit. The surfboard probably just looks like an hors d'oeuvre. Bite wound will be large and ugly.

1. Assess condition of victim.
2. Pack wound with clean bandage. Apply pressure to stop bleeding.
3. Keep victim warm to help prevent shock.
4. Evacuate to medical facility.

Guitar fanatic's fingertip

Changing chords hundreds of times daily toughens up your fingertips. But if they get too beat up or cracked, initiate treatment:

1. Soak your fingers in warm water for 20 minutes.

2. Apply a lanolin-based lotion.

3. Plunge them into a bowl of rice to toughen them up again.

CHAPTER 64
DEAL WITH DISASTER

Hypothermia, Pacific style

The Pacific Ocean doesn't vary much from its normal range of 50–55°F all year long. Immersion in cold water leads to hypothermia in about 15 minutes. Once your core body temperature falls, it falls fast. Below 90°, you're unconscious. Below 80°, you're dead.

What to do if you go overboard

(**1**) Hope you're wearing a life jacket. (**2**) Assume the Heat Escape Lessening Posture (HELP). Hold the inner sides of your arms against your chest, press thighs together, raise knees to your chest. (**3**) Hug and huddle. If several people have fallen out of one boat, get cozy. Share body heat. (**4**) Keep your head up. Besides the obvious fact that you won't be able to breathe otherwise, you lose heat quickly from your head. (**5**) Hope that you haven't been drinking. Alcohol dilates blood vessels, exacerbating heat loss. (**6**) If you don't have a life jacket, tread water. This also helps keep you warm.

Hypothermia treatment

(**1**) A victim just out of the water requires assessment. Shivering, numbness, pain from the cold may be early signs of hypothermia. (**2**) Remove wet clothing. (**3**) Cover victim with a blanket. (**4**) Give warm drinks, preferably sweetened.

For more severe hypothermia

(**1**) A victim of severe hypothermia may be shivering less, but speech could be slurred to the point where the person appears drunk. Loss of reasoning may occur. Lips turn blue. Victim may be unconscious or nearly unconscious. (**2**) Medical assistance required.

(**3**) Besides blanket, warm with sleeping bag or additional blankets.   (**4**) Use CPR if necessary.

How to avoid wildfires, or survive them

If you live in a rural, wooded area, you need to take precautions against wild fires.

(**1**) Say no to a flammable cedar roof. Try steel. It lasts forever and is fireproof.   (**2**) If you build in a fire-prone area, try nonflammable building materials, such as brick, concrete, or river rock.   (**3**) Develop a sprinkling system/plan that allows you to reach at least a hundred yards from your home.   (**4**) Most important, create a defensible space around your house by using fire buffer zones:

ZONE I *(within 50' of house)*	ZONE II *(50–100' from house)*	ZONE III *(100–150' from house)*
MOIST AND TRIM. Use only low-growing, succulent, fire-resistant plants. Water regularly. Turf or perennials: rhodies, iris, mountain laurel, daylilies.	LOW AND SPARSE. Here you want more low-growing stuff that will tolerate drought. Suggested shrubs: Oregon grape, holly, serviceberry, redflower currant, sumac.	HIGH AND CLEAN. Trees are OK in this zone, but no branches should be within 10 feet of the ground. Keep trees thinned and trimmed. Best trees are Oregon white oak, maple, quaking aspen.

*What to do if you are
trapped in a forest fire*

(**1**) Look for the two Rs: roads and rivers. They may afford escape routes. (**2**) Do not head uphill. Fires race up hillsides rapidly. (**3**) Stay low, beneath choking smoke, which makes oxygen scarce. (**4**) Get into a pond or lake. Swim away from fire if possible. (If nothing else, this will flameproof your clothing.) (**5**) If there is no escape route, a space blanket may afford some protection (this is one reason you should keep one in your day pack). Get into a ditch. Curl up, with space blanket tucked all around you. Hope fire misses you.

*Tools for
fighting wildfires*

SHOVEL

PULASKI. THE PULASKI LOOKS LIKE AN AX THAT'S BEEN CROSSED WITH A HOE

FIRE-RETARDANT SUIT

HELMET

What to do if a tsunami wave hits

A tsunami may strike the coast within minutes after a coastal quake. If you feel an earthquake when you are on the coast:

(**1**) Drop, cover, and hold on if you're indoors.   (**2**) If you're outside, avoid falling objects. Bricks don't have much give.   (**3**) Avoid danger points: the beach, low coastal areas including the lowest parts of coastal cities, mouths of rivers that meet the ocean.
(**4**) Immediately move in and up. Inland, and uphill, as far as you can. Don't wait for official warnings.
(**5**) Stay away from the coastline. A tsunami will typically be a series of waves, not a single wave. Do not, repeat, do not return to the beach after the first wave passes. Additional waves may come hours later.
(**6**) Return to beachside areas only after an all-clear is given.

FACTOID │ The Good Friday quake of 1964 that struck Alaska generated tsunamis all down the coastline, smashing bridges in Cannon Beach, Oregon, and killing 11 people in Crescent City, California.

How to survive being trapped in a mosh pit

(**1**) Extend arms in front of you to create breathing room.   (**2**) Yell "I'm a Republican" and moshers will panic and flee.   (**3**) If you are hoisted and passed overhead, keep surfing until you see an exit sign. (**4**) Undercut one slam dancer, and others will stay clear.   (**5**) If all else fails, Kenny G fan club ID will cause moshers to recoil in disgust.

"I'm a Republican"

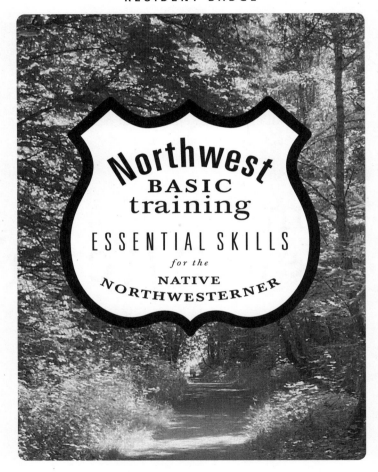

Northwest
BASIC
training
ESSENTIAL SKILLS
for the
NATIVE
NORTHWESTERNER

*Awarded if you accomplish at
least six of the following:*

❑ Summit 10,000-foot-plus mountain.

❑ Catch a salmon. (With your bare hands.)

❑ Cut up a 12-foot tree in less than an hour...using
  only a scout knife.

❑ Live in a snow cave for two days.

❑ Prepare vanilla lattes for entire family at
  Thanksgiving.

❑ Use a chain saw to carve a statue of an eagle.

❑ Give up red meat for seafood.

❑ Sell your minivan and commute by bicycle.

❑ Retrace the route of Ken Kesey's magic bus.

❑ Make plaster cast of actual Bigfoot print.

*How to acquire your Northwest Basic Training
Mastery Badge:*

Send a completed checklist with a self-addressed, stamped envelope to:
SASQUATCH BOOKS, 615 SECOND AVE, SUITE 260, SEATTLE, WA 98104.

ACKNOWLEDGMENTS

Thanks to:

Novella Carpenter and Gary Luke
at Sasquatch Books

Researchers Eric Eiden and Sharon Hollomon

The Eiden and Hollomon families for their support

Steven Williamson of Rogue Brewing

Chef Charlie Flint of Hudson's Grill

Brett Wilkerson and the staff at the Heathman Lodge
in Vancouver, Washington

Ed McLarty of Portland Running Company

Oyster Barn in Lincoln City

World Forestry Center

U.S. Forest Service

American Red Cross

U.S. Geological Survey

Portland Art Museum, Native American Studies Department

Mike Smith, Ken Chitwood, Tim Parker

Everyday Music

Dave Krysinski, golf pro at Semiahmoo Resort, Blaine, Washington

Emily Cahal of Addictions Piercing and Tattoos

Don Nelson, River City Fly Shop

Dan Price, Mr. Walking Stick

Cal Burt, outdoorsman and snowshoe craftsman

Alex Crick

Crown Records

Cowboy poets Ben McKenzie and Rudy Gonzales

Todd Gilmer at Pacific Trail Outerwear, Seattle

The Albany Timber Carnival

Seattle Aquarium

Don Ornsby of Wilsonville Coffee Co.

David Marshall, wildlife biologist

Brian Boucher

Bob Logue

Ellen Whiteside, masseuse

MASTER AND IDENTIFY

Fig. 1,965.

Fig. 1,96

SHORT.

SIMPLE.

TO THE POINT

Fig. 2,057.

Beginner's Guide:

HOW TO APPRECIAT

Fig. 2,032.

Coffeehouse Lingo

Fig. 2,046

Fig. 2,049.

HANDY TRICKS